DRY LAND

WINNING AFTER 20 YEARS AT SEA WITH THE
PITTSBURGH PIRATES

CHARLIE WILMOTH

DRY LAND

CHARLIE WILMOTH

2014

First Printing: 2014

ISBN-13: 978-1495983986
ISBN-10: 1495983986

www.twitter.com/wilmothc

U.S. trade bookstores and wholesalers: Email charliewilmoth@yahoo.com

Cover photography and design: Honor Forte

Introduction

You're not supposed to go to a carnival to feel miserable. And yet here I am, surrounded by thousands of baseball fans whose team has caused them two decades of pain. They're here – at a carnival – to sit down, cross their arms, cock their eyebrows, and wait for their team to tell them next year will be different. Some part of each of them will believe it, but a bigger part won't. They'll go home distrusting the motives of the men in charge, questioning the talent of many of the players on hand, and wondering what they did to deserve a generation of awful play. They're not *supposed* to feel miserable, just as you're not *supposed* to go to a baseball game to feel miserable. And yet that's exactly what many fans of the Pittsburgh Pirates say they do.

December 14, 2012 is warmer than it should be, one of those late-autumn days where you can pretend it's mid-March. And in Pittsburgh, it might as well be. The Steelers are still in playoff contention, but they're in the midst of a disappointing 8-8 season. The Penguins are caught up in the NHL lockout, their players banished to sparsely attended practices at Southpointe. And today, baseball is in the air. Or something like it, anyway.

    I stand in line at PirateFest, the Pirates' offseason festival, surrounded mostly by adults who wear their team's gear but exhibit no real excitement. At 4:00, the doors open, and we spread through Pittsburgh's convention center like a puff of smoke coughed into a

Dry Land

room. Many line up to collect player autographs. Others glance at booths where middle-aged men sell baseball memorabilia and younger ones hand out 2013 schedules for the Bucs' minor-league affiliates. The Pirates give out free calendars in plastic bags, which most guests probably don't need but carry around awkwardly. There are T-shirts and game-used jerseys hanging from makeshift cubicle walls, and if you wander to the far end of the convention floor, you can find weirder bits of Pirates-related flotsam, like ancient unopened cereal boxes with Roberto Clemente's picture on the front. Children climb on enormous inflatable floats and eat free hot dogs. ROOT Sports and 93.7 The Fan, which carry Pirates games on television and radio, respectively, broadcast from the event. Players and announcers occasionally stroll by, usually with fans stopping them every few steps.

The line to get in was long, but the convention floor is huge, and the event isn't yet nearly at capacity – it won't fill up for another couple hours, when the nine-to-fivers arrive. A makeshift stage, where the Pirates' front office will later answer fans' questions, is now empty. A salesman from the Pittsburgh *Tribune-Review* offers free copies of that day's paper, trying, perhaps a little too zealously, to get the attention of passers-by. Batting cages, bounded by black netting, go unused. The room feels like an airport at 5:30 AM – it's quiet, and sparsely populated, but it's clear that will soon change.

I am 33 years old. I've been writing about the Pirates since I was 24. I arrived, fresh-faced, from the minors almost nine years ago, and now I'm a crusty vet with a slow bat and a one-year contract. Most of the players who walk by are younger than I am. The Pirates were already in the midst of their 12th straight losing season when I started writing, and at least right now, they're still losing.

Writing began as a hobby, and now it is work. Well, sort of. I still like it, but I have to think of it as a job. Otherwise, I'm just a 33-year-old driving three hours to catch glimpses of a bunch of rich 26-year-olds I watch on TV.

4

Charlie Wilmoth

There are, of course, many Pittsburghers for whom a winter baseball carnival can simply be a winter baseball carnival, or for whom a night out at the world's most beautiful ballpark can be uncomplicated fun, even if the home team loses. But there are also plenty who take all the losing seriously, and for whom the idea of a Pirates-themed celebration is an oxymoron. These are, naturally, the people most likely to come to PirateFest.

We love to pretend the Pirates make us miserable, but they don't, really. We have *some* semblance of free will. To a serious baseball fan, changing one's rooting interest or giving up on the sport entirely feel like unnatural acts. But they *do* seem like legitimate responses to true misery. Some fans have drifted away over the years, with serious fans becoming casual fans, and casual fans becoming non-fans. But there are still thousands who stick around.

It is 2012. The Pirates have had 20 straight losing seasons. A 20-year losing streak is difficult to put into perspective, in part because no other major American pro sports team has ever had one. With their 17th straight losing season in 2009, the Bucs topped the 1933-1948 Philadelphia Phillies for the longest such streak in history. Since then, they've been in a league of their own. The Pirates tantalized us by competing well into the summers of 2011 and 2012, only to fall apart each time, nurturing their streak nearly to drinking age. And so here we are, celebrating a team that has been losing since before some of its minor-leaguers were even born. It's party time in Pittsburgh.

I'm at PirateFest, in part, to talk to serious Pirates fans I wouldn't find on the internet. I'm thinking these people are mostly older, which might be wrong, but when you're trying to talk to random strangers, you have to have *some* sort of plan. I'm feeling apprehensive about approaching people – I'm not particularly outgoing, and anyway, PirateFest has just opened. I figure that if you're going to stand in line to enter a carnival, you probably have better things to do immediately after you enter than to talk to some blogger.

Dry Land

That turns out to be wrong. The first fan I interview is a 70-something retired steelworker named Robert who I find sitting by himself near a concession stand. He seems ready to pounce, as if he's been waiting *years* for someone to ask his opinion of the course the Pirates have charted.

I ask if he's interested in seeing Pirates president Frank Coonelly and general manager Neal Huntington answer questions later that evening.

"No," he says, flatly. "I can give the same answers they give. It's all P.R."

He then launches into a long list of grievances against the Pirates' front office.

"They just cannot evaluate ballplayers. They drafted a catcher, [Tony] Sanchez, number one three years ago. What happened to the guy?" Robert asks. The Pirates selected Sanchez fourth overall in 2009, and he's still in the minors.

"Their biggest weakness is catching," he continues. "They could have had Mark Wohlers [Matt Wieters] about three or four years ago."

Coonelly and Huntington hadn't yet been hired when the Pirates passed on Wieters in 2007, but I'm in no mood to stop Robert, who opines about the quality of shortstop play throughout the National League before bashing the front office yet again.

"The good players they got weren't signed by this regime," Robert says. "[Andrew] McCutchen, [Neil] Walker, and the third baseman [Pedro Alvarez] were all signed by [Dave] Littlefield."

Littlefield, Huntington's predecessor, did draft McCutchen and Walker, but Alvarez was Huntington's first pick in his first draft in 2008. In fact, Alvarez, who was represented by the ultra-aggressive agent Scott Boras, was the sort of expensive, high-upside draft pick that Littlefield never would have selected.

Robert is, in a way, very well informed – he can recall specific details not only of games and Pirates players (which you'd expect from a fan who's been a season-ticket holder since 1994, as Robert has), but also of draft picks and bits of Pirates news that happened away from the field. He also plainly cares deeply about the team. Whenever he makes a mistake, though, it's at the expense of the front office. And note the misplaced fascist/authoritarian connotations of the word "regime."

None of this is accidental. Pirates fans are an argumentative bunch, constantly branding one another "apologists" or "yinzers" and characterizing Huntington and Coonelly as despots, as if they came to occupy their offices on Federal Street as the result of a military coup. (An objective assessment as of December 2012 would have suggested that, for all of Huntington and Coonelly's faults, they merely were average executives not quite up to an incredibly difficult task. They weren't exactly Chairman Mao and Idi Amin.) As I speak to more fans, I will find that, if I'm having trouble getting an interview subject to open up, I can simply ask what he or she thinks of the Pirates' front office. 90 percent of the time, I find myself in the midst of a rant, and I know that eventually I'll be looking awkwardly to the side, trying to find the right time to turn off the recorder and say my goodbyes.

Later, I speak to Simon, a former government employee now in his 60s who's clinging to his season tickets, he says, despite a lack of interest in the current team.

"It's not the modern-day Bucs," he says. "You can see the alumni members, radio crews, nice guys." Simon also cites the Pirates' Field Days, in which season-ticket holders can take batting practice and shag flies on the PNC Park grass, as a reason he keeps buying.

Still, he often finds the ballpark experience itself depressing. "You go to PNC Park, Phillies, Cubs ... there are more [fans of visiting teams] wearing their colors at PNC Park than Pirates fans wearing Pirates [colors]."

Of course, there may be some *Pirates* fans not wearing their team's gear. "I was ready to break out my colors last year," says Simon. But he ultimately decided not to. "I got these new logo leather jackets, hats. They ain't earned it."

Dry Land

For the most part, PirateFest is good, clean fun, and an outsider might be able to spend a half hour strolling about without realizing there's a problem. It's as close as many fans will get to some of their favorite players, who participate in game-show-style entertainments, sign autographs, and mill about the convention center floor wearing their Pirates jerseys over casual button-down shirts. The previous year, Bucs backup catcher Michael McKenry eagerly greeted fans at the door as I entered. He was so short that it took me a minute to realize who I was suddenly talking to, and it was a pleasant surprise once I did. Pirates fans have never really blamed the players, at least not on a personal level, for the way the last two decades have gone, and PirateFest offers a great opportunity for fans to meet them.

This evening, even the Q+A session with Coonelly, Huntington and manager Clint Hurdle turns out to be mostly polite, as it usually is, even though one of the papers has published a list of accusatory questions for fans to ask. It's difficult to be impolite in front of a thousand people. But beneath the event's surface swims anger and frustration and pain. And when the fans finally file out of the convention center tonight, they will head home not only with positive memories of shaking hands with Hurdle or Neil Walker, but also with a peculiar blend of hope and suspicion and bitterness that grows riper with each passing year.

These are the Pirates' most loyal customers. And for once, they are about to be rewarded.

Chapter 1

The worst aspect of the Pirates' streak of 20 straight losing seasons is that, within the world of professional baseball, the Pirates matter. Or they *should* matter, even if the economic structure of Major League Baseball keeps telling them they don't. The Pittsburgh Alleghenys joined the National League in 1887 and changed their name to the Pirates prior to the 1891 season. They've played in Pittsburgh continuously since then. Some of their players have been among the greatest ever, including Honus Wagner, Pie Traynor, Paul Waner, Arky Vaughan, Ralph Kiner, Bill Mazeroski, Willie Stargell and Barry Bonds. In the 1960s and 1970s, in particular, the Pirates were one of baseball's iconic teams. Mazeroski's walk-off home run to end the 1960 World Series is one of the sport's biggest moments. And then there's Roberto Clemente, who delivered 3,000 hits for the Pirates before dying in a plane crash while trying to deliver supplies to earthquake victims in Nicaragua. Clemente is a hero not only in Pittsburgh, but also in Latin America.

"It's not the Miami Marlins. It's not the Diamondbacks," says Neil, a 50-year-old Pirates fan who grew up in New Jersey, admiring the team from afar before moving to Pittsburgh and becoming a season-ticket holder in the midst of the streak.

"It's kind of like the Canadian teams in the NHL. The Toronto Maple Leafs actually matter to the league," Neil says. The Pirates are a key part of baseball lore. For any club to have 20 straight losing seasons is bad enough, but for a team with the Pirates' proud

Dry Land

tradition to have 20 straight losing seasons is, as Neil puts it, "a travesty," at least within the framework of baseball history.

The Pirates have won two world championships since Mazeroski's walk-off, one in 1971 and another in 1979. In the 1970s, they had nine winning seasons and won their division six times, led by Clemente and then Stargell. The 1970s Pirates featured Dock Ellis throwing a no-hitter on LSD. One of their top hitters, Dave Parker, was a drug-abusing slugger nicknamed "The Cobra." They wore ridiculous gold pillbox caps. In 1979, they rallied around Sister Sledge's disco song "We Are Family." In other words, the Bucs of the 1970s were as flamboyantly freaky as the decade itself, and they won and won and won some more. The decade was marred by Clemente's tragic death in 1972. But otherwise, the 1970s provided nonstop, druggy excitement.

The 1980s were the morning after, and in ways more literal than one might think – in 1985, much of the team found itself at the center of a national cocaine scandal. The high was gone, and the 1980s went by slowly, painfully. In 1984, the Bucs lost 87 games; in 1985, they lost 104, and in 1986, they dropped 98. I attended my first Pirates game during this period, sitting in the absolute top row of the giant concrete bowl that was Three Rivers Stadium. Each row seemed to be perched high above the one below it, positioned at what seemed to my six-year-old eyes to be an absurdly steep angle. I sat with my back glued to my seat, fearful that, if I stood up or leaned too far forward, I'd fall, perhaps all the way down to the field. Most Pirates fans probably felt they already had.

After 1979, the Bucs didn't win their division again until 1990, and Bucs fans were faced with ugly performances like Jose DeLeon's remarkable 2-19 record in 1985. Or Jim Winn's vanishing strikeout rate the same year, when he somehow whiffed just 22 batters in 75.2 innings.

But in the lean years of the mid-1980s, the Bucs also laid the groundwork for their successful early-1990s seasons. They picked Barry Bonds sixth overall in the 1985 draft, then acquired future ace

Doug Drabek in a deal with the Yankees after the 1986 season. In the meantime, they'd also reacquired third baseman Bobby Bonilla from the White Sox after losing him in the Rule 5 Draft. Then, at the start of the 1987 season, they picked up not only athletic center fielder Andy Van Slyke, but also catcher Mike LaValliere and pitcher Mike Dunne, when they shipped veteran backstop Tony Pena to the Cardinals.

Led by Bonds and Van Slyke (and manager Jim Leyland, whom the Bucs had hired to his first big-league managerial job before the 1986 season), the Pirates began to improve beginning in 1987, when they won 80 games. They won three straight division titles from 1990 through 1992, losing in the NLCS each time.

The last NLCS ended with an infamous 3-2 loss in Game 7 against the Braves. Orlando Merced knocked in a run with a sacrifice fly in the first, and Jay Bell doubled in the sixth and came home on Van Slyke's single up the middle to put the Pirates up 2-0. Meanwhile, Drabek pitched eight scoreless innings.

In the bottom of the ninth, though, Braves third baseman Terry Pendleton led off with a double, then moved to third as second baseman Jose Lind struggled with a hard grounder from David Justice. Drabek then loaded the bases by walking former Pirates first baseman Sid Bream, who represented the winning run.

Stan Belinda relieved Drabek and gave up a sacrifice fly to Ron Gant. He then walked Damon Berryhill, moving Justice to third and Bream to second, and got Brian Hunter to pop out. And then up came Francisco Cabrera, a first baseman, catcher and minor-league veteran of no particular distinction who had received only 11 regular-season plate appearances with the Braves that year. Cabrera lined a single past the shortstop and into left field, and Bonds' throw home was just a little off-line. After Justice scored the tying run, Bream came lumbering home. LaValliere stood in front and to the right of the plate, then fielded Bonds' throw on one knee and spun back, swinging his arm over the plate just after Bream's lower body crossed it. Bream was safe, and the Pirates' season was over.

Dry Land

It was a tough loss made tougher by Bonds' imminent departure – the Giants signed him away that December with a $43.75 million contract. Drabek, meanwhile, signed with the Astros for $19.5 million. But Pirates fans didn't know that Cabrera's hit and Bream's slide would mark the beginning of an awful new era for the franchise, a perfect storm of mismanagement and small-market poverty and plain-old shit luck.

"Some of my earliest memories are being four and five years old, watching my dad watch Pirates games on TV and asking him questions about them," says Pat Lackey, who was born in 1985 and who now runs the excellent Pirates blog Where Have You Gone, Andy Van Slyke?

"After the Pirates lost to the Braves, [I remember] telling my dad the next morning, 'Well, it's okay, we'll be back to the playoffs next year. We'll win it next year.'

"It wasn't really until I got to high school that I started to understand all the different factors that were conspiring against them, both [from within] themselves and the conditions in baseball."

Lackey followed the team through high school, but really came back to the Pirates as a student at Duquesne. He had stopped playing the game himself and, after having grown up near Hermitage, now lived within walking distance of PNC Park. With his physical proximity to the team, and with Duquesne's high-speed internet, the Pirates were more accessible to Lackey than ever before.

Lackey started his website in 2005. Like many Pirates blogs at the time, WHYGAVS often seemed like a coping mechanism, or a way of wondering why rooting for the Pirates even made sense. He repeatedly considered quitting – once in 2007 (more on that later) and once after the Pirates' collapse in 2011. Ultimately, he stuck with it because, despite the Pirates' shortcomings, baseball was a form of escapism.

"Part of what sports is about is that everything else in life is very serious," he says. "I'm very logical about things, and I don't have to be logical or serious about the Pirates if I don't want to. Why would you ever watch a baseball team that has treated the fans

14

as bad as the Pirates have over the past 20 years? The answer is that it doesn't matter, because it's just a baseball game."

That's probably the clearest and most sensible answer to this book's central question. Why do we do this to ourselves? We do it in part because it's baseball – it's a beautiful game most of the time, even the way the Pirates play it. And while it's the National Pastime, it's also merely a pastime, a nice complement to joyously long, languid summer nights, and nothing that needs to be more significant than that.

But really, though. "It doesn't matter, because it's just a baseball game"? It certainly doesn't *feel* that way.

In 1993, Francisco Cabrera's career began to unravel. He got 83 more at bats with the Braves that year, but never played in the majors again. In 1995, he appeared briefly with the Braves' Triple-A team in Richmond, and also played for the Thunder Bay Whiskey Jacks, a team in the independent Northern League based in Ontario. The following year, he played for several teams in Mexico. He also suited up for clubs in Japan, the Dominican Republic and Taiwan before winding up, in 1998, with the Albany-Colonie Diamond Dogs, in the independent Northeast League. He made $1,400 a month, and among his teammates were a football coach and a grad student.

"You know what's funny?" Cabrera asked *Sports Illustrated* that year. "They had me and Javy Lopez ready to pinch-hit, and they picked me. Javy Lopez is a star in the majors. The guy who threw the pitch was Stan Belinda. Stan Belinda is still in the majors."

Cabrera, however, was not. He'd ruined the Pirates' last playoff run for two decades, and then fallen off the face of the earth.

I was a Pirates fan as a boy, in the Bonds / Van Slyke years, when the Pirates made the playoffs for the last time. I got to attend about one game at Three Rivers each year, and I watched an occasional weekend game, but my main connections to the sport were through numbers, which I pored over on the backs of baseball cards and in

Dry Land

the pages of the Wheeling *News-Register*. By the time I reached high school, the Pirates' losing streak had already been going for several years. I grew more interested in rock music and politics, and I drifted away from the game. I spent lunch hours splayed out in a hall-hallway, writing song lyrics that I'd later record on a boombox. I quit playing basketball and joined the debate team in my sophomore year. After that, I was too preoccupied with adolescent rebellion to make room for sports, which I felt were conformist. I focused much of my energy on playing the guitar and the violin. And so I missed much of the early part of the streak, fiddling while the Pirates burned.

The departures of Bonds and Drabek were only the beginning. Baseball players don't last forever and certainly no longer play for one team forever, and the fabric connecting the Pirates to their early-1990s winning ways began to tear. The Bucs dealt second baseman Jose Lind to the Royals after the 1992 season. They released Mike LaValliere in early 1993. Van Slyke, by then in his early 30s, left after the 1994 season and played for the Orioles and Phillies in one more year after that as he dealt with decline and injuries. And in April 1995, the Pirates made one of their worst decisions of the streak, releasing 28-year-old Tim Wakefield, who immediately caught on with the Red Sox, pitching brilliantly for Boston in the first season of a 17-year career there.

Following the 1996 season, their fifth straight losing campaign, the Bucs traded first baseman and outfielder Orlando Merced to the Blue Jays in a nine-player deal that netted slugging catching prospect Craig Wilson and middle infielder Abraham Nunez. They also sent Jay Bell and Jeff King – half their infield – to the Royals for third baseman Joe Randa and three other players. Four years after the Pirates' last playoff appearance, they were nearly unrecognizable.

As the roster changed in the mid-1990s, the Pirates' ownership changed as well. The Pirates found themselves in limbo, playing their home games in a small market and in a dump of a ballpark, and after a strike prematurely ended the 1994 season, the Pirates were in dire financial straits. It appeared they might leave town entirely, which would have been a tremendous loss, given the team's long history in Pittsburgh. But in early 1996, Kevin McClatchy, a Sacramento native whose family was in the newspaper business, led a group of investors who purchased the Pirates from Pittsburgh Associates for $95 million, with the help of a loan from the city. McClatchy kept the team in Pittsburgh, and beautiful PNC Park was built on his watch, if not on his dime.

McClatchy's goals were ambitious. "This is a growing process for us. We're not going to turn this thing around in one year," he admitted in early 1996. Nonetheless, he said, "We have a five-year plan that will probably get us to the playoffs in two years." Strangely, the "playoffs in two years" part of the plan nearly came true, and McClatchy's "five-year plan" *still* became a running joke.

The destruction of the Pirates' roster from their last winning season was nearly complete by the time McClatchy took over, leaving the Bucs with … well, not much. The 1997 Pirates had the smallest payroll in baseball, and they were an odd mix of promising or semi-promising young players (including outfielder Jose Guillen; starters Jason Schmidt, Esteban Loaiza and Francisco Cordova; and catcher Jason Kendall, who became the greatest Pirates player, or at least their longest-running star, during the streak) alongside also-rans and not-quite-veterans like Al Martin, Kevin Polcovich, Tony Womack and Dale Sveum.

Not much was expected, particularly after the trades of Bell, King, Merced and starting pitcher Denny Neagle. But the mix worked far better than it should have, given the talent involved, and the Pirates surprisingly contended in a very weak NL Central division. In late June, the Bucs were 36-43, and they appeared headed toward their usual dismal finish. But they won seven straight before the All-Star break and ended the first half leading the NL Central by a game, despite a microscopic $9 million payroll.

"All anybody wanted to talk about was these no-name Pirates," Womack, who represented the Bucs in the All-Star Game,

Dry Land

told the *Post-Gazette*. "Talking about that with the media was better than being selected. I told the media, 'Man, we're having fun! We came out of nowhere.'"

Immediately after the break, the Pirates lost their first two games of a four-game set against the Astros, falling back into second place in the process. But the next day, Cordova and Astros starter Chris Holt traded zeroes through the first several innings. The game was still scoreless in the eighth, when Cordova got Bill Spiers and Brad Ausmus to ground out. Tim Bogar followed with a popup to short right field, and Kevin Young caught it over his shoulder. Cordova still hadn't allowed a hit. He got two grounders and a fly ball again the next inning, finishing a nine-inning no-hitter.

As the game headed to extra innings, Cordova had thrown 121 pitches. Manager Gene Lamont replaced him with Ricardo Rincon, who walked Derek Bell (then an Astro) with one out but got Spiers and Ausmus to end the threat. Kendall then reached base on a one-out walk, and after Guillen flied out, Turner Ward followed with a walk of his own. Mark Smith came on to pinch hit for Rincon, and Astros reliever John Hudek left an 0-1 fastball out over the plate. Smith smashed it to left, and the Pirates won 3-0, moving back into a tie for first with a ten-inning no-hitter.

That win put the Pirates at 44-45. They reached .500 the next day, retaking the NL Central division lead in the process, then beat the Mets to cross the .500 threshold. They dipped below the Astros shortly thereafter and spent much of the next month hovering a couple games below .500, generally tailing first-place Houston by five or six games. In late August, though, they took five of six from the Padres and Giants to swoop within three games of the division lead. The buzz surrounding the Bucs grew louder in late August, when they acquired shortstop Shawon Dunston in a rare in-season trade for a veteran. Dunston made his Bucs debut on September 2 and homered twice as the Pirates moved within a game and a half of the Astros.

18

They tailed off immediately thereafter, losing eight of their next ten and never again getting closer than three-and-a-half games out of first, and they finished 79-83. But it had been a surprisingly inspiring season, and the '97 "Freak Show" Bucs are still fondly remembered in Pittsburgh.

The same can't be said of the 1998 edition, which lost 93 games. After the '97 season, the Pirates left Joe Randa unprotected in the expansion draft as the Diamondbacks and Devil Rays prepared for their debut seasons. Randa was cheap, he was coming off a strong year, and he was still relatively young, and so it was no surprise that the Diamondbacks eventually picked him. That was frustrating in itself, but it was the Pirates' reaction that hurt most. After a couple months of Freddy Garcia and Doug Strange at third base, the Bucs promoted 19-year-old Aramis Ramirez, who had spent the previous year in the Class A+ Carolina League. Unsurprisingly, it would be three more years before Ramirez would really blossom, a timeline that might have been delayed because of the Pirates' decision to promote him before he was ready.

Not that the rest of the '98 team was much better. The Bucs scored the third-fewest runs of any team, finishing behind even expansion Arizona, thanks to poor seasons from Al Martin, Ramirez, and just about everyone who didn't have a full-time role. It was a frustrating, if not surprising, return to irrelevance.

After the season, the Pirates did deal Rincon for Brian Giles in a lopsided trade that gave the Bucs four-and-a-half years of one of the best hitters in the National League. Led by Giles, Kevin Young, and a fluke season from starter Todd Ritchie, the '99 Bucs came close to .500, going 78-83 and scoring nearly as many runs as they allowed. It was a breakout season for Giles in particular – the outfielder posted a 1.032 OPS, good for fifth in the National League. As bad as the Pirates would be throughout the decade of the 2000s, they always did have at least one slugger, usually Giles or Jason Bay, who the Bucs acquired when they traded Giles. The Pirates were bad, but they could have been a lot worse.

Dry Land

Giles, alas, was only part of the picture. If the post-Freak Show Pirates were to have any success, they would need to depend on their core of young starting pitchers. Unfortunately, the Pirates traded Jon Lieber to the Cubs for the disappointing Brant Brown before the 1999 season, and Lamont leaned too hard on the pitchers who remained. In 1999, for example, Lamont had Jason Schmidt, perhaps the most promising of the bunch, throw at least 120 pitches seven times. Unsurprisingly, Schmidt missed most of the following season after undergoing surgery to fix a torn rotator cuff and frayed labrum. Lamont also pushed former No. 1 overall draft pick Kris Benson, particularly in 2000; Benson missed the entire 2001 season with Tommy John surgery.

The '99 season also included the trade of Jose Guillen to the Devil Rays. Guillen had been a frustrating player for the Bucs, but that had more to do with the Pirates' nonsensical approach to player development than with Guillen's talent. In the Freak Show season, the Pirates had promoted Guillen, then just 20, all the way from Class A+ to the big leagues. They would have been far better off, in the short and long terms, if they had just given the playing time to another player in the organization, or even a waiver claim. As it stood, Guillen continued to struggle in Tampa Bay and Arizona for a few years before finally emerging as a minor star in Cincinnati in his late 20s. It isn't hard to imagine that he could have played some of those star-caliber years with the Pirates, if only they'd been patient with him.

The Pirates weren't just handling their young players badly. PNC Park was set to open in the 2001 season, and in preparation, the Pirates signed veterans to contract extensions that would hamstring the team for years to come.

In April 1999, the Pirates inked infielder Pat Meares, a good defensive player but a complete zero as a hitter, to a four-year, $15 million deal that would not begin until the following season. This was especially bizarre, since Meares was already in the Pirates organization, having signed a one-year, $1.5 million free agent contract for 1999. Then, a month before the two parties agreed to the

20

four-year deal, Meares suffered a hand injury that the Pirates misdiagnosed, thinking it was a sprain. The injury caused Meares to miss most of the 1999 season, and the contract hadn't even kicked in yet. So, to summarize, the Pirates acquired Meares for $1.5 million on the open market. Then, after he had done little in a Pirates uniform but hit in spring training and get hurt, the Bucs decided he was worth four years at $3.75 million apiece.

Meares played regularly in 2000 and hit poorly, although no worse than he had with the Twins in 1998. In 2001 he appeared in 86 games and hit a miserable .211/.244/.304, leading to a farce the following season in which Meares and the Pirates disagreed about whether he was healthy enough to play. Meares spent 2002 on the disabled list, and he filed a grievance against the Pirates, wanting them to release him (but still pay his guaranteed salary), so that he could play elsewhere. The Bucs then tried to recoup the money they wasted on Meares with an insurance claim. Whether he was healthy enough to play, and when, remains unclear, but even leaving the injury aside, his decline from a vaguely-palatable middle infielder to a running joke was one the Pirates should have anticipated, or at least prepared for, given his age.

Also in 1999, the Pirates had signed first baseman Kevin Young to a four-year, $24 million deal that would kick in beginning in the 2000 season. $6 million a season isn't much for a baseball player now, but for the Pirates in 1999, it was an enormous figure that guaranteed Young would be an important part of their immediate future. As with Meares, though, the problem was that Young was an aging mediocrity, not a star. After he signed the deal, he put up a career year in 1999, a year the Pirates had already controlled. And then, as he entered his thirties, he fell off the face of the planet.

This was, again, a scenario that should have struck the Pirates as fairly likely at the time of the contract. In 1996, before his late-1990s heyday, the Bucs had actually released Young. He then headed west to play for the Royals, until they, too, cut him, after the 1996 season. Young should not have been considered a core player. Instead, he was a veteran in the midst of a peak that would likely be

Dry Land

brief. As with Meares, Young's failure with the Pirates was connected to his health – he had knee issues throughout the contract. But it was never likely that Young's deal would turn out well.

On his way out of town, though, Young made a point to blame not his knees, but Pirates fans, suggesting that they showed insufficient enthusiasm for the Bucs' losing ways. "A lot of things can snowball on you there, whether it's the fans or the scorekeeping," Young told the *Post-Gazette* in 2003, several years after he had last performed at even a reasonable level, and less than two months before being released. "At this point, I don't really give a damn. ... When we're at home, and we don't have any home-field advantage, you better believe I'm going to say something about it."

Also in preparation for the opening of PNC Park, the Pirates signed their two true stars, Brian Giles and Jason Kendall, to long-term deals as well. Unlike the Meares and Young contracts, these weren't obviously terrible ideas. Giles' $45 million deal turned out to be a bargain, and having him under contract helped the Pirates get good talent back when they shipped him to San Diego a few years later.

There was a case to be made for the Kendall extension at the time, too. Following the 2000 season, the Bucs agreed to pay Kendall $60 million in a six-year deal that started in 2002. It was, clearly, a risk – catchers tend not to age well, and the Pirates had already worked Kendall hard, having him catch in 147 games in 2000. The deal was also the biggest in the team's history. But through age 26, Kendall's abilities to hit for average, draw walks and steal bases made him an historically unique player for a catcher – BaseballReference.com lists Kendall's top comparable through 2000 as Hall of Famer Mickey Cochrane. And the Pirates were only locking Kendall up through age 33, an age through which a terrific catcher might well remain productive.

"If I didn't believe we were going to win here, I wouldn't stay here, no matter how much money they gave me," Kendall told the press after the signing. "It's going to happen here. I've just got that feeling."

22

As it turned out, the contract wasn't nearly the disaster many Pirates fans considered it to be, but it also probably wasn't what either party was hoping for. (The ultra-competitive Kendall did, of course, collect $60 million, but he also allegedly greeted new Pirates players to Pittsburgh by saying, "Welcome to hell.") Kendall's on-base percentage shrank by 77 points in 2001, and in the years that followed, his power almost completely abandoned him, likely thanks in large part to a thumb injury. He was very effective in 2003 and 2004, posting on-base percentages near .400 and more than earning his salary, but the Pirates dealt him to Oakland for pennies on the dollar anyway.

In any case, the Pirates' decisions as they prepared for the opening of PNC Park did them few long-term favors. They chose to pretend they had a competitive core in place rather than actually building one. "We took over this franchise, and it was in disarray. You didn't have the depth in the minor-league system or the major-league roster," McClatchy's former business partner Jay Lustig told the *Post-Gazette* in 2013. "I would say the biggest mistake that the McClatchy era might have made is we should have come clean and said, hey, we're going to rebuild and do it right."

The Pirates lost 93 games in 2000, thanks in large part to a pitching staff and defense that allowed nearly five-and-a-half runs per game. Kris Benson was the only starter who had a good season, and terrific offensive performances from Giles, Kendall and journeyman outfielder John Vander Wal weren't enough to rescue a mediocre offense.

Worse, Aramis Ramirez, Jason Schmidt and second baseman Warren Morris, all young players who had looked like they might be important parts of the Pirates' future, struggled. Top outfield prospect Chad Hermansen, whose rookie-league manager had once said could "walk on water," got caught in a rip tide, struggling to control the strike zone at both the majors and the minors. So did Jimmy Anderson, a young pitcher who was considered a building block at the time but wasn't very good to begin with. Anderson was

Dry Land

living proof of what baseball was missing before the development of sabermetrics. He had widely been considered a top prospect after a superficially impressive season in the minors in 1996, but if he'd come along ten years later, prospect writers would have ignored the 2.77 ERA and focused on his mediocre strikeout and walk numbers and unimpressive stuff. As it stood, the Pirates gave Anderson about three full years' worth of starts to prove himself. Unsurprisingly, he never did.

Before the 2000 season, McClatchy had told the press the Pirates might win 90 games, "as long as everything goes right." Of course, that wasn't a responsible projection – "To think this team had a chance to win 90 games, somebody must be dreaming a lot," as Giles later told reporters. And even the modest, mismatched talent the Pirates had on hand wasn't all it had been cracked up to be. Hermansen broke camp with the Pirates that season, but played poorly and got demoted to Triple-A in May. The *Post-Gazette* reported that, by the summer, he was receiving phone calls from former big-league teammates telling him the clubhouse atmosphere in Pittsburgh was so toxic that he should feel grateful to be in the minors.

Hermansen also disagreed with the Pirates' decision to alter his hitting approach after he arrived in the majors. "No one in the organization had ever said much to me about my hitting. Then, after I finally made it to the big leagues, they wanted to change me," he told the *Post-Gazette.* "I must have tried five different stances with my hands in different positions. They wanted me to use more of an upper cut in my swing. But that backfired on me. It just made my swing longer." Prior to the 2000 season, Hermansen had played five years in the minors and never posted an OPS lower than .814 at any level. But right after the Pirates started actively coaching him, he fell apart, struggling to hit even in the minors – his .688 OPS at Triple-A in 2000 was completely out of character with what he had done before.

Perhaps the Pirates were trying to fix issues that would have caused problems for him no matter what, and surely Hermansen's coaching was not the only cause of his downfall. But it was still a bit odd that, after the firing of Gene Lamont following the 2000 season, the Pirates decided their new manager would be … Lloyd McClendon, Hermansen's hitting coach. McClendon had no managerial experience above the Class A+ level at the time.

In other words, as the Pirates headed toward the opening of PNC Park in 2001, they were nowhere near where they needed to be. They had a beautiful new retro ballpark that was about to earn a reputation as one of the very best in sports. But they lacked a baseball team to play in it. And, hours before the park was set to host its first regular-season game on April 9 of that year, Willie Stargell, the top power hitter and spiritual leader of their '79 World Series team, passed away from a stroke at age 61. It was a bad omen.

Chapter 2

With the opening of their new ballpark, 2001 was a crucial year for the Pirates. Coming off a 93-loss season, though, they might have felt like they were in one of those dreams where you're about to give a presentation, and you suddenly realize you're naked – vulnerable, afraid, unprepared. And so, on a rainy day near the end of spring training, Brian Giles took his clothes off, had a teammate tape a sign bearing his number 24 to his back, and took batting practice in his birthday suit.

"Nudity is how I deal with things when there are a lot of problems," Giles told *Sports Illustrated*'s Jeff Pearlman. "When times are bad, you have to do something to snap everyone out of it."

In 2001, after eight years at the helm, Cam Bonifay's tenure as the Pirates' general manager was nearing its logical conclusion, and the Pirates' streak of losing seasons was already nearly a decade long.

Bonifay's decisions, and his comments about them, were fascinating. He showed little indication that he could turn the Pirates into a winning team, but at least he was unintentionally entertaining.

"This pitching staff has a lot of moxie," the GM told the *Post-Gazette* in April 2001. "I just like the club. Their tenacity. Their ability to fight the odds. I think we've got a bunch of guys who are battlers and who struggled and had to go through some down times. I'm looking forward to all of them rebounding and being part of a team, instead of worrying about individualism."

Dry Land

Moxie! Tenacity! *The ability to fight odds!* Bonifay was still looking for his first winning season in his ninth year on the job, and his plan for the team still sounded like a deleted scene from *Rudy*. Bonifay's attempts to be positive amounted to an admission of failure. What is a general manager supposed to do but create a team that has good odds to win?

"There's been a lot of times we've been predicted to be a bad club," said Bonifay. "Sometimes, the way you play, if you get lucky, you'll prove all the geniuses that made those determinations wrong."

As it turned out, the geniuses were right. Bonifay lost his job in June, and the Pirates limped to a 100-loss season. It turned out that a team that leaned heavily on scrubs like Jimmy Anderson, Pat Meares, Abraham Nunez and Omar Olivares didn't have *quite* the moxie to chasten those know-it-all pundits.

It wasn't hard for even a new fan to see through Bonifay's public statements. Nor was it hard to see *why* he had failed. Signing Pat Meares made no sense, even at the time. Neither did signing fading veteran outfielder Derek Bell to a $9.75 million deal. Bell played one season for the Pirates and batted .173. The following spring, he notoriously declared that he would go into "Operation Shutdown" if he had to compete for a job. The Pirates released him and ate the remainder of his contract, and he retired to live on his yacht, prompting local columnist Mark Madden to quip, "Derek Bell becomes the ultimate Pirate: Lives on a boat and steals money."

Bonifay was well intentioned and had his strengths. Despite a series of failed first-round picks, his drafts were respectable, especially after he hired scouting director Mickey White. Bonifay also made a few good trades, like the Ricardo Rincon / Brian Giles deal and the 2000 swap of reliever Jason Christiansen for shortstop Jack Wilson. But Bonifay had little money to work with, and even less of a clue what to do with it.

I wandered back into baseball fandom as a young adult, and I naturally returned to the Pirates, whose brief period of good play in the early 1990s hit just at the peak of my period of preteen baseball-card-collecting geekiness. This time, though, the Pirates interested me precisely *because* they were bad. Not just bad – ridiculous. Their self-evidently stupid behavior zapped me with the self-righteousness that powers arrogant young men. Between their financial disadvantages and their management's incompetence, it was hard to imagine a future in which the Pirates could win, but this was good, in a way. I felt smarter than the men who ran a big-league baseball team. Go me!

Having grown up in West Virginia and gone to college in Virginia, I had few other Pirates fans around who shared my grievances against the team, and that only increased their intensity. The internet was relatively young then, and there weren't blogs about the team, or much intelligent chatter at message boards, at least not that I was aware of. My main sources of news were ESPN.com, which rarely had any Pirates news at all, and the website of the *Post-Gazette*, Pittsburgh's biggest paper. The main Bucs writer at the *Post-Gazette* was Paul Meyer, who penned a weekly Q+A column in which he tried to justify every absurd move the Pirates made. And so the Bucs' ineptitude took on an urgent quality – not only was my team being run poorly, but very few people even seemed to be talking about it.

There was, surely, grumbling at the ballpark, around Pittsburgh, and perhaps even in certain corners of the internet, but I wasn't around to hear or see it. And so I seethed when, after the 2002 season, Meyer ludicrously predicted that the Bucs would sign free agent Jim Thome, then coming off a 52-homer year with the Indians. (Signing Thome would have been such a dramatic change from the way the Pirates usually did business that to suggest they might acquire him felt like a cruel joke.) And I took particular umbrage at the Pirates' treatment of Craig Wilson, a slugger who tied MLB's record for pinch-hit homers in his 2001 rookie year but was used sparingly, even though the Pirates' other first basemen and right fielders were routinely among the worst in the league. *I could run this team so much better*, I thought.

Dry Land

Compounding my exasperation, and my delusions of grandeur, was the ideological battle going on within baseball at the time. A few general managers had begun using trendier, smarter statistics to find players they perceived to be undervalued. On-base percentage was in; batting average was out. Strikeout-to-walk ratio was in; pitcher wins were out.

One effect of the rise of these new statistics – collectively known as "sabermetrics" – was that, in the first decade of the 21st century, more and more teams began to favor them. The game improved as a result. But another effect was that fans like myself began to appreciate advanced statistics as well. In the early aughts, sabermetrically inclined fans and traditionalists took to battle on baseball websites. In hindsight, there was plenty of arrogance on display on both sides. But as a young man who was plenty arrogant himself, that didn't bother me. And as awareness of new statistics spread, sabermetrically inclined fans had more talking points at their disposal, and the internet gave them a convenient new platform.

Within the game, the apparent conflict between sabermetrics and scouting was, ultimately, partially a false one. As the first decade of the 2000s wore on, it became clear to most teams that there was much to be gained from both approaches. But one lasting effect of the sabermetric movement is that it taught teams, and their fans, the value of a dollar. Sabermetrics wasn't just about numbers, but about finding hidden advantages, and spending money wisely. Sabermetrics and the internet therefore helped hold general managers' feet to the fire in a way that had never before been possible. Increasingly, if a team did something silly, it would hear about it, and it would hear about it *immediately*.

Sabermetrics wasn't merely about new statistical approaches. It was about fans acquiring new tools to express their opinions. Some of those opinions were about teams signing players who didn't fit the sabermetric paradigm. But some of them were simply about decisions by general managers that defied common sense. For example, if a GM paid heavily for a player who was barely better than a player he might have signed to a minor-league contract, his team's fan base would lambaste him. No longer was it assumed that there was some unseen good reason why a GM's inexplicable move actually made sense. Sabermetrics made fans more knowledgeable, and less trusting of authority, and as a result, the game became more interesting to me.

Partially as a result of sabermetrics, the quality of baseball's general managers rose throughout the decade, as GMs either got smarter or were replaced by brighter talents. Had Bonifay been dismissed, say, two years later, when acceptance of sabermetrics was more wide-spread, the Pirates might have wound up with a good GM. Instead, what they got was former Montreal Expos and Florida Marlins executive Dave Littlefield, who made Bonifay look like Stephen Hawking.

Bonifay, at least, had been *trying*, and he had at least some idea how to find good young players. He and his staff didn't have any idea how to develop those players, or turn them into a team, but if he could have done so, he would have. And as bad as many of Bonifay's decisions were, the Pirates' streak was relatively young then.

"That was before the misery had totally set in," Bucs Dugout writer Wilbur Miller says. Fans still tended to view the team somewhat hopefully, still talking among themselves about potential acquisitions and trades as if those moves might one day help.

"There were actually real conversations [among fans], like, 'Gee, this might get better.' The team had a pretty good core of players," says Miller. "There wasn't this pervading sense of total frustration that came later."

As the Pirates' streak of losing seasons grew, Bucs fans began to congregate on the internet in greater numbers, sharing more and more information. My blog and Where Have You Gone, Andy Van Slyke? were among the first Pirates blogs to develop readerships, alongside now-forgotten names like Honest Wagner, Batting Third, Bucco Beyond, and Romo Phone Home. Brian O'Neill of the *Post-Gazette* began posting saber-friendly articles under the name "The

Dry Land

Stats Geek." Other Pirates fans gathered at message boards, like OnlyBucs.net and PittsburghSports.net, and on listservs. And the quality of discourse around the team took a big leap forward in 2005, when Dejan Kovacevic took over for Meyer at the *Post-Gazette* and began reporting in an open-minded way, completely different from the screaming-head persona he eventually developed as a columnist. Kovacevic took angry fans seriously, questioned the team in an intellectually honest manner, and provided fodder for critical discussions of the Pirates.

One of the strangest, and best, developments on the web during that period was the emergence of Miller's Pirate Player Profiles website, which contained biographies of every player in the Pirates' system, all the way down to the Gulf Coast League. (The site still exists, and is now housed at Pirates Prospects.) Back then, the site was built from the crudest HTML, and you could find it by pointing your browser at a URL that began with "mywebpages.comcast.net."

Miller told me later that he created it not even as an internet site, but as a series of posts to a listserv that he at one point offered to the group's members as a set of Microsoft Word documents. But he wrote authoritatively not only about the Pirates' big-leaguers, but about Class A players I'd never even heard of. He'd seen most of them play, and his keen understanding of how to put minor-league stat lines in context was rare at the time. Miller's withering reviews of Littlefield's drafts, in particular, helped shape hardcore Pirates fans' opinions of the Bucs' farm system long before the rank and file figured out there was a problem.

"The concept of building a team by trading away veterans for minor-leaguers just interested me because, like anybody at that point in time, I couldn't help wondering, 'How in the hell does a team that doesn't have a lot of money compete?'" says Miller.

The quality and scope of what Miller was doing was probably unusual *anywhere*, but most of the rest of Bucs fans' route to the internet was fairly normal. Fans of most teams probably took similar paths to fan communities and websites to follow their teams on the web. What made the situation unique, though, was that they were finding a home on the internet precisely as Littlefield was destroying the team. It was possible to see his destruction of the Pirates from close range, and as we watched it happen, we no longer needed to feel like we were alone.

Among Littlefield's first tasks as general manager was to negotiate with Bonifay's picks from the 2001 draft, and if we had known what to look for, we might have seen even then that the long-term interest of the team wasn't his top priority. Bonifay had selected Stephen Drew, a Georgia high school shortstop and the brother of then-Cardinals star J.D. Drew, in the 11th round that year. Stephen Drew later told Kovacevic that, before Bonifay was fired, the Pirates had been making a serious effort to sign him. After Littlefield took over, though, negotiations fizzled. Drew headed to Florida State, then emerged three years later as the top position player in the 2004 draft; the Diamondbacks took him in the first round, and he quickly emerged as a good big-league regular.

Nonetheless, Littlefield's incompetence wasn't obvious at first. Even an idiot can look like a reasonable GM for a couple years after following someone like Bonifay. As a GM, cleaning up someone else's mess isn't that difficult, and if you do, the fans, or at least the well-informed ones, will like you well enough for a while.

The Pirates' on-field results during Littlefield's first couple years were miserable, not that those years were primarily Littlefield's fault. The Bucs lost 100 games in 2001, as Brian Giles' usual strong season and a breakout year for Aramis Ramirez weren't nearly enough to offset the struggles of Jason Kendall, Kevin Young, Pat Meares, rookie Jack Wilson, and much of the pitching staff. Then, in 2002, they lost 91, as their everyday lineup only included two players – Giles and Craig Wilson – who posted above-average seasons with the bat.

Littlefield's moves through his first couple of years were a mixed bag. He shipped Jason Schmidt and John Vander Wal to the Giants for pitcher Ryan Vogelsong and outfielder Armando Rios, a deal that turned into a disaster – Schmidt blossomed in San Francis-

Dry Land

co, and neither Vogelsong nor Rios ever took root in Pittsburgh. But Littlefield also dealt starting pitcher Todd Ritchie to the White Sox for future rotation regulars Kip Wells and Josh Fogg, probably his best trade. He also beefed up the 2003 team by signing veterans Reggie Sanders, Kenny Lofton, Matt Stairs, and Jeff Suppan on the cheap.

Meanwhile, the farm system, then headlined by prospects acquired during the Bonifay era, was, at least, modestly promising. Catcher J.R. House, shortstop Jose Castillo, and pitchers Sean Burnett, Bobby Bradley and John Van Benschoten were the big names, but further down, the system also had Jose Bautista, Nate McLouth, Bronson Arroyo, Chris Young (the pitcher) and a number of other future productive big-leaguers. Littlefield swore he didn't want the flow of young talent to stop, and it was a couple years before it was obvious he hadn't meant that.

"With Littlefield, there was a lot of rhetoric about the farm system," Miller says. "There wasn't a lot of information available, and it took time to figure out how completely absent the commitment to the farm system was."

Late in the 2003 season, Littlefield traded Giles for a package that many fans found underwhelming at the time, but that I liked – he got young lefty Oliver Perez, who at least ended up having one outstanding season, and future star outfielder Jason Bay.

By that point, though, it was becoming clear that something was wrong. A month before the Giles trade, Littlefield had shipped Lofton and Aramis Ramirez to the Cubs for virtually nothing. Ramirez, barely 25, blossomed into a star with the Pirates' division rivals. That trade had more to do with the Pirates' ownership and financial situation than with Littlefield, but it was becoming clear that the Bucs were not to be taken seriously, regardless of who was in charge.

"The Ramirez trade was kind of a watershed, because I think that's when they gave up making legitimate efforts," Miller says. "The trade itself was incredibly idiotic. It was obviously dictated by financial mismanagement on McClatchy's part. But from that point on, I just thought that Littlefield was like a scam artist."

Littlefield's first two years had also included several bone-headed moves, including losing Arroyo and Young, who became solid starting pitchers for other teams, for virtually nothing. (Arroyo went to the Red Sox after Littlefield exposed him to waivers, and Young headed to Montreal in exchange for a reliever who never pitched an inning for the Pirates.) It wasn't until the end of the 2003 season, though, that Littlefield's tenure got *really* silly. Due to a series of bizarre decisions, five of the first six players taken in the Rule 5 Draft that winter were Pirates minor-leaguers.

The Rule 5 Draft isn't like the better-known June amateur draft, in which it's generally possible for the first five or ten teams to draft a star. In the Rule 5 Draft, teams can protect 40 players on their major-league roster, and many minor-league players aren't eligible. So it's rare for players selected in the Rule 5 Draft to go on to great things.

Unsurprisingly, then, the players the Pirates lost didn't come back to bite them too badly. (The only player of the five who ended up having a long career was Jose Bautista, who the Pirates reacquired the following year.) But the losses demonstrated that Littlefield was grossly unprepared. The Pirates were a bad team; the Rule 5 Draft, which prevents clubs from hoarding major-league-ready talent in the minors, was designed to *help* teams like the Bucs. Littlefield easily could have removed any number of unproductive players from the Pirates' roster to clear space to protect his young-sters. But he didn't. And the reaction around baseball was clear – on the ballroom floor where the draft took place, as one team after another swiped a Pirates minor-leaguer, baseball people began openly laughing.

Give Littlefield some credit, though – at least that was funny. Or, you know, funny to *someone*. Most of the key moments in Little-field's tenure had to do with how stupid or absurd they were. For pure comedy, the Littlefield era was hard to top.

Dry Land

Over the course of about a thousand baseball games, there will be real moments of inspiration. Like the Pirates' amazing comeback from a six-run deficit with two outs in the ninth against Billy Wagner and the Astros (capped by Brian Giles' walk-off grand slam) just a couple weeks after Littlefield took the job in 2001. Or utilityman Rob Mackowiak hitting a walk-off grand slam in the first game of a doubleheader in May 2004, then a game-tying two-run shot in the ninth inning of the second game.

Mostly, though, the Littlefield era will be remembered for losing, for his awful decisions, and for things like first baseman Randall Simon hitting a racing sausage with a bat. In July 2003, the Bucs, by then completely out of the playoff race, were in Milwaukee. Several Pirates, wearing baggy gold throwback uniforms, stood on the dugout steps as a group of young people dressed as sausages ran around the field as part of the between-inning entertainment. As they approached the Pirates' dugout, Simon leaned over the railing and took an overhead swing at one of the sausages (actually a 19-year-old named Mandy Block), hitting the top of her costume. There was no visible reaction from Simon's teammates, perhaps because they already knew of his tendency to swing at everything. Block and another sausage toppled, leading then-Brewers manager Ned Yost to comment, "I just looked over and saw our wieners in a wad."

Neither sausage suffered injuries more serious than scraped knees, but the Milwaukee County Sheriff's Department cited Simon, who paid a $432 fine. It was a bizarre scene, and a sad one – the incident drew the Pirates a rare bit of national attention, and for what? The Bucs soon traded Simon to the Cubs, for whom he knocked a key home run in Game 3 of the NLCS against the Marlins. For the Cubs, Simon hit a playoff homer. For the Pirates, he hit a sausage. Yep, that sounds about right.

Beginning in late 2003, my sense of superiority from feeling smarter than the Pirates' management began to fade. It became increasingly clear that the Bucs would remain near the bottom of the NL Central for the foreseeable future. There was no point in going down with the ship. As the hopelessness of the situation set in, I began to hunt for another team to follow, one more worthy of my attention.

The Oakland Athletics. The Toronto Blue Jays. The Boston Red Sox. I tried to root for all of them, but it never felt real. In early 2004, as I planned to move to San Diego for grad school, I tried to root for the Padres. But there was nothing on the line. I didn't feel the connection I felt to Pittsburgh, a city that, growing up in northern West Virginia, had felt like New York and Paris and Tokyo all rolled into one. I saw the colors of other teams and felt nothing. Even after I gave up on rooting for the Padres as my primary team, I'd come home from school and watch their games with the kind of detachment one might expect of a film critic, or a scientist. But when I saw a team in black and gold, I knew it was mine, however flawed it might be. For better or worse, I was stuck with the Pirates.

So I started a blog. After a year, I probably had about 20 regular readers; a year after that, I had perhaps a hundred. Meanwhile, the Pirates' comedy of errors continued. For 2004, which turned out to be their 12th straight losing season, the Bucs re-signed Simon, and also inked outfielder Raul Mondesi, third baseman Chris Stynes, and closer Jose Mesa. Mesa was passable, but the rest were embarrassing busts, and the team had to terminate Mondesi's contract when he left the team to go to the Dominican Republic and didn't come back. Later in the season, the Phillies offered future star first baseman Ryan Howard for free-agent-to-be Kris Benson, and Littlefield turned it down. Kovacevic later reported that Littlefield did so because he felt the Pirates had a Ryan Howard of their own in prospect Brad Eldred, who went on to hit a total of 15 big-league home runs.

The 2004 team won 72 games. But even that was better than the 2005 edition, which won just 67. Before the season, the Pirates had traded Jason Kendall to the Athletics for reliever Arthur Rhodes (who they then sent to Cleveland for outfielder Matt Lawton) and starter Mark Redman. Kendall ended up declining steeply after the trade, but the Pirates were clearly motivated to deal him primarily because of his salary, not his performance. It was a depressing trade for the Bucs, who gave up a star and received two role players in return.

To replace Kendall, Littlefield, with characteristic absurdist flair, traded pitching prospect Leo Nunez for 39-year-old catcher Benito Santiago. Nunez had earned the nickname "Little Pedro" – as in Martinez – for his small frame and good stuff. The odds were against him ever becoming a star, but the Pirates were in no position to be trading a talented young player for a 39-year-old. Nunez (whose real name was later revealed to be Juan Carlos Oviedo) blossomed into a good, cheap reliever with the Royals and then the Marlins; Santiago played just six games for the Pirates.

The few signs of progress in 2005 were mostly crammed into the first two-and-a-half months of the season. On June 11, the Bucs beat the Devil Rays 18-2 thanks to huge nights from Jose Castillo and Oliver Perez. The win put the Pirates at .500 for the first time that late in a season since 1999, and the fans treated it as a milestone, celebrating as if their team had just clinched a playoff berth.

I was at PNC at the time, cheering along, happy to have something to celebrate. But I felt pathetic. Perez's case demonstrated perfectly how weak these .500 Pirates really were – he had ten strikeouts in that game, but his velocity and mechanics were clearly worse than they had been the previous season, when he had looked like one of the game's brighter young talents. The Bucs were just a bad team playing a hair better than usual, and they were beating up on one of the very few teams in baseball that, at least at the time, was in even worse shape than they were.

The Pirates' season went downhill soon after. Later in June, Perez, already suffering through an ugly season, had a bad start against the Cardinals, kicked a laundry cart in frustration, broke his toe, and landed on the disabled list for two-and-a-half months.

Cart punt aside, the causes of the Bucs' problems were clear from a cursory glance at the roster. Their primary catcher was Humberto Cota, who hadn't hit much in the minors and who'd spent the previous year as Kendall's little-used backup. Their main first baseman was Daryle Ward, a minor-league signee. As an Astro in 2002, Ward had become the first player at PNC Park to hit a ball into the Allegheny River on the fly, but since then he'd flamed out with the Astros and Dodgers. The Bucs' primary centerfielder was Tike Redman, who they were playing mostly because they still hoped his obviously fluky 2003 stretch run wasn't actually a fluke. (At the end of the season, the Pirates finally replaced Redman with Chris Duffy, who had a similarly fluky stretch run; the Pirates proceeded to make the same mistake with Duffy over the next two seasons.) And the starting rotation consisted of frustrating talents in Perez and Kip Wells, plus three pitchers in Redman, Josh Fogg and Dave Williams who were No. 4 starters at best.

In other words, the Pirates still weren't a serious team, and their .500 season through mid-June was an illusion. And so it was no surprise to see them lose five in a row and vanish from relevance shortly thereafter. The team fired Lloyd McClendon near the end of the season, eventually replacing him with former Dodgers manager Jim Tracy.

2006 was just as bad. The season began with actor Michael Keaton – Batman – taking to the press to criticize the Pirates' ownership right before throwing out the first pitch at their home opener. "I fear they will take advantage of the good will of the people who continue to show up," said Keaton, a Pittsburgh native. The Pirates were so bad, even the guy throwing out the first pitch at their home opener publicly bashed them. The highlight of baseball in Pittsburgh that year wasn't even one the Pirates earned – PNC Park hosted the All-Star Game, and Jason Bay won a starting spot in the outfield in a shameless ballot-stuffing campaign orchestrated by the Pirates. (I conducted a half-serious "Stop Voting For Bay" campaign at Bucs Dugout, on the grounds that the team didn't deserve any extra good publicity, but alas, the Pirates won out.)

Before the 2006 season, Littlefield pointlessly signed former Freak Show Bucs third baseman Joe Randa, now a grizzled veteran, as well as outfielder Jeromy Burnitz. Even before the season, Randa didn't look like an upgrade over the younger Freddy Sanchez, and

Dry Land

after Randa got hurt early on, the Bucs were faced with the indignity of watching Sanchez take over the job and chase the NL batting crown (which he eventually won). While Sanchez was batting .341 in late May, Littlefield told the media that Randa would remain the starting third baseman once he returned. Fortunately, the Pirates didn't stick to that plan. Sanchez forced their hand, and he emerged as a minor star in Pittsburgh. But Randa and Burnitz were the faces of a team that had decided it would rather be old than good, or even interesting.

One of the nice things about living in California at the time was that I could hide my disgust at the team I followed. My grad-student friends and I almost never discussed sports, which kept me from allowing my frustration with the Pirates to infect my personal life. Friends who had known me for years would express shock upon learning I had a blog about baseball. I followed the Pirates almost exclusively through the internet, and I liked it that way.

The series the Pirates would play in San Diego each year was the one time I didn't feel my secret was safe. The Pirates games I attended at PETCO Park felt strange, like traveling overseas and running into an acquaintance from high school. In 2006, the San Diego series was in late September, when the Pirates were beyond irrelevant. I went to the park and watched the Padres' Chris Young face the Bucs. Young took a no-hitter through six innings, then seven, and I began to root for him, excited at the opportunity to see an historic event in person, and amused at the possibility of Dave Littlefield being embarrassed by a pitcher he'd traded away.

With the Padres leading 6-0, Young took his no-hitter through the eighth, whiffing Jason Bay and Ronny Paulino and inducing a grounder from Xavier Nady. But in the ninth, Young, approaching 100 pitches, began to fall apart, and it became clear, even from my vantage point high above the action, that his pitches weren't going where they were supposed to. He got Ryan Doumit to line out to deep right, but then walked Jose Bautista. And then up came Randa, who smashed the longest home run I'd ever seen him hit. Other than the fact that it ruined Young's no-hitter, it was completely irrelevant. I was furious.

That I was rooting for Young to complete the no-hitter, and that I was upset that Randa broke it up, were typical of how many Pirates fans followed their team. To fans of most teams, my thinking might seem strange, even blasphemous, but this is how a fan thinks when he's been conditioned by 14 years of failure. Before the game, the Bucs were 65-88; it didn't matter much whether they finished with, say, 94 losses or 95. I'd go to the park and watch the Pirates, but if I could exchange a victory to be present for a slice of baseball history, well, that was an easy decision. And if that bit of baseball history was ruined by a superfluous veteran hitting an irrelevant home run, that was a shame. In fact, any success Randa might have would simply reinforce the team's view that it was pursuing the right strategy.

"The Pirates were about to be avalanched in irony with the best possible reminder of the management's ineptitude, getting no-hit by a man they traded for absolutely nothing," Pat Lackey wrote at the time. "Randa's homer only indirectly served to further the agenda of the bastards that run this charade of a baseball team. Somewhere, probably in a dark room, Littlefield is telling the Nutting family, 'See, I told you he was worth the money!'"

The 2006-2007 offseason was actually somewhat promising. Littlefield acquired Adam LaRoche, a relatively young first baseman who could hit and looked like a good fit for PNC Park, for the modest cost of closer Mike Gonzalez and middle-infield prospect Brent Lillibridge. It was a strong move to improve the Pirates' lineup, even if it wasn't franchise changing. And the Bucs got off to a 12-12 start in April.

But then they went 11-18 in May and continued to go downhill in June, when they played so badly the frustration seeped into the team's interviews with the press. "I fucking hate this," pitcher Ian Snell declared. "I fucking hate losing. I hate when the team doesn't bring out its full potential. If they want to fine me, fine me. I don't care, because this is getting stupid." LaRoche and other Pirates hitters struggled. (Throughout his Pirates career, LaRoche hit terribly in the early months, then turned on the gas in summer and fall, when the Bucs' season was already functionally over.) It quickly became clear that the team wasn't going anywhere.

With the fourth overall pick in the amateur draft that month, the Pirates took lefty Danny Moskos, who projected as a reliever in the majors, instead of top catching prospect Matt Wieters. Taking a reliever with the fourth overall pick would almost never make sense, but especially not for a terrible team, and with a consensus star-caliber player available. The Pirates then blew many times the money they saved in bypassing Wieters on a bizarre trade-deadline deal for fading starting pitcher Matt Morris, who they would pay $14 million over the next year and a half.

The *Post-Gazette*'s Paul Meyer had dutifully reported on Moskos' 95-MPH velocity and "wipeout" slider, but when I saw Moskos pitch for Clemson right after the draft, he threw 87-89 MPH, topping at 91 MPH, and didn't have anything resembling a "wipeout" breaking ball. He didn't look like a first-round pick at all, let alone a No. 4 overall pick.

Morris, meanwhile, was almost 33, and even a casual glance at his statistics revealed that he was nowhere near the pitcher he had been when he'd starred for the Cardinals years before. His strikeout rate was declining for the sixth straight year, coinciding with a drop in his average fastball velocity from about 92 MPH in 2002 to less than 88 MPH in 2007. And, of course, even if Morris had somehow reversed those trends, the only upside for the Pirates was that they'd win 70 games in 2008, instead of 67. As it turned out, Morris posted a 6.10 ERA for the Bucs down the stretch in 2007, and then was even worse in five starts in 2008, forcing the Pirates to release him.

To say that Littlefield wasn't trying at that point would probably be too kind. He was trying to do *something*, like a junkie willing to do anything for his next score. Littlefield likely hoped the Moskos and Morris moves would provide short-term fixes that would pre-

Charlie Wilmoth

vent the Pirates from firing him. And, in typical Littlefield style, the moves didn't even work as short-term fixes. Wieters arrived in the majors before Moskos and made a much bigger impact when he did, and Morris' career was effectively over by the time the Pirates traded for him.

By this point it was blindingly clear that, as bad as Bonifay had been, Littlefield was far worse. Compare Littlefield's behavior in his last few months on the job to the way Bonifay had explained his approach as of October 2000, months before being fired.

"We're not going to take a more polished pitcher who has a chance to be a middle reliever or No. 5 starter if there's a more raw high school kid out there who could be a No. 1 or No. 2 starter," Bonifay had told the *Post-Gazette*. "I don't care if that player takes longer to develop. I might not be here to see it happen, but I want the next general manager to be able to see it."

Bonifay had meant it, too, picking dozens of high school players, including Stephen Drew and Zach Duke, in the 2001 draft, shortly before he was dismissed. In contrast, Littlefield was not only a talentless GM, but a selfish one.

After the Morris trade, I considered quitting blogging. If I hadn't had an audience at that point, however small it might have been, I probably would have. The deal took place shortly before the trade deadline, but it wasn't actually reported until a half hour later. I sat at a computer until 20 minutes after the deadline, waiting to see if the Bucs had done anything else. Then I left. When I returned the next morning and read about the Morris deal, I felt a profound sense of deflation.

My team was in the midst of a 15-year losing streak, and it showed no signs of stopping. There was more out there – my career, time with my family, finding a girlfriend. Hell, on paper, any number of more mundane things, like learning to cook or vacuuming my apartment, would have been better uses of my time than watching the Pirates. And yet I kept going. I never really did learn to cook. I probably didn't vacuum enough. I wasn't in particularly good shape. And my girlfriends put up with my habit, somehow

Dry Land

never noticing I was a masochist. The games stayed on, and I tuned in for one slap in the face after another.

Somehow, there are *thousands* of fans who didn't turn off the TV when Randall Simon hit that millionth grounder to first, or when Ronny Paulino dropped another throw home, or when Ian Snell threw yet another middle-middle fastball to Albert Pujols. Why did they stay? As of 2012, some of them weren't even alive when the Pirates last had a winning season. How did they make it to 2013?

I'm interested here in the hardest of the hardcore fans, the season-ticket holders and the message-board posters and talk-radio callers. Being a hardcore fan of a team means investing a significant percentage of your energy. When you do so and your team wins the World Series, the payoff is obvious. But what about when your team *never wins anything*? How can you love a team that doesn't love you back?

Let's say you hated high school. Those four years probably seemed endless. The Pirates' losing streak lasted five times that long. Or let's say you hated high school so much you *murdered someone* after you graduated. The average maximum sentence for murder and nonnegligent manslaughter in state courts in the U.S. is 20 years and four months. So if you had *killed someone* after Bream's slide in 1992, the streak would probably have still been going when you got out of prison.

Pirates fans are no longer the same people they were when the streak began. Those who were middle-aged when it started are now old. Those who were young are now middle-aged. And many of today's young adults weren't even alive in 1992.

The number of serious Pirates fans is small compared to the number of serious fans of most other teams. But it is still a large number, in an absolute sense. In most populations that include thousands of people, there will be extraordinary diversity of thought, and Pirates fans are no exception. In the course of writing this book, I frequently felt I had stumbled upon an important tenet of Pirates fandom, and then the very next person I interviewed

44

would say something that contradicted the point I thought I wanted to make. Perhaps you, the reader, are yourself a serious Pirates fan. You will probably see aspects of your fandom represented here, along with some traits with which you don't identify.

There is nothing inherently virtuous about being a Pirates fan. As we'll see, Bucs fans can be as petty as those of any other fan base. Besides, baseball is just a form of entertainment we enjoy in the relatively rarefied spaces of state-of-the-art ballparks, and in the living rooms of well-made houses in our developed nation. Most of us are lucky even to be here, in America, and to have the leisure time to root for our shitty baseball team. Ultimately, the agony of watching our shitty team lose is not real agony, and our loyalty to our shitty team is not real virtue. Working tirelessly to feed the hungry is virtuous. Rooting tirelessly for a baseball team is not, regardless of how selfless it might feel. And although Pirates fans' circumstances are strange, the fact that the Pirates still *have* fans after 20 straight years of losing is not.

"Kansas City still has fans. *They* haven't all quit," Wilbur Miller points out. "I don't think it's anything other than just normal that you'd have a core that would stick around, [along with] a lot of people that wouldn't."

So there's nothing special about Pirates fans?

"Nothing, other than that they have a better understanding of … misery than most other fans," Miller says.

Watching baseball, for most of us, is merely a hobby, regardless of how painful it might be. This isn't to say that rooting for the Pirates during the streak was easy, or that it didn't hurt. It clearly did, as we'll see. But we should try to maintain perspective. I want to understand us. I do not want to romanticize us.

Nonetheless, the Pirates forced their fans into an unusual situation. And when the Bucs finally won again in 2013, there wasn't a fan base that deserved it more.

Chapter 3

As I began writing this book in 2012, I asked readers of my blog to pick one word to describe their relationship to the Pirates. Here's a sampling of their answers.

Loyal

Proud

Optimistic

Analyst. "I like baseball as a statistical case study first, and as a sport second. ... Additionally, when I got into baseball for real ... the Pirates were rebuilding for real, and it was fascinating."

Consistent. "I've followed and rooted for the Pirates consistently through good times (70s, early 90s, now) and bad (the last 20 years)."

These are words that fans of many teams might use. The loyal, proud fan who sticks with his or her team through good times and bad. The analytical baseball fan who thinks about the sport in terms of statistics. There are Yankees or Braves or Mariners or Dodgers fans who would happily describe themselves using these terms.

Dry Land

Few Yankees or Dodgers fans would describe themselves using *these*, however.

Volcanic. "That's the best word to describe the love I feel for them. What I like to think is that I and we as a community are party [to] something unique in sports history. I've lived through the streak … and I know for a fact that when we do finally win, what we have gone through will make it a feeling of satisfaction and elation and VOLCANIC joy that no other fan of any franchise in sports history can quite understand."

Masochistic. "19 years of losing and hoping this will be their year."

Delusional. "Because every April, no matter what, I always think the Bucs have a chance to win it all."

Sucker. "For the past two decades, I've had tempered expectations for the Pirates … until February/April. Then I get spring fever and start believing that those several things could finally fall the right way and the Pirates can contend."

Hardened. "When you meet people and mention you like baseball, the next question that normally follows … is, 'Who is your team?' The past 18 years, after I said the Pirates, it was followed by laughter and joking. Just recently, though, probably [in the] past three to four years, that laughter has been replaced by a look of sorrow and compassion. The one you give people when you find out they have a deathly sick relative."

Helpless. "I've never even considered not being a Pirates fan. It ain't why, why, why, it just is."

It's true that there are many fans of the Cubs or Red Sox, for example, who might describe themselves as "masochistic" or "helpless." These people are whiners. Don't listen to them.

Since 2000, the Cubs have had six winning seasons and gone to the playoffs three times. Before 2013, the Pirates hadn't had a winning season since "Whoomp! (There It Is)" topped the charts. The Cubs haven't won a World Series in a century, but many Pirates fans weren't alive for the Bucs' last championship either, and Cubs fans haven't had to deal with endless summers of irrelevance the way Pirates fans have. The Red Sox, meanwhile, have won three championships since 2004. Cubs and Red Sox fans lounged in kiddie pools while Pirates fans swam the English Channel.

The Pirates fan's predicament is not *totally* without comparison, and later, I'll explore potential connections between Pirates fandom and that of the Baltimore Orioles, Kansas City Royals and Cleveland Browns. But the Bucs' situation is the absolute last stop on the road to despair. It's too remote for any but the unluckiest souls.

Whether or not to root for a baseball team is, fundamentally, a choice. Even though my attempts to root for the Padres and the Athletics didn't take, I could have just dropped out, stopped reading box scores, stopped watching games.

But I didn't. For the hardcore fan, following the Pirates is a choice, but it doesn't *feel* like one. And so it's no surprise that Pirates fans often turn to the rhetoric of addiction to explain what the Pirates do to them. As the Bucs limped to a 57-105 finish in 2010, Pat Lackey read David Foster Wallace's novel *Infinite Jest*. Lackey found himself identifying with the novel's hero Don Gately, a gargantuan former criminal and recovering Demerol addict.

"They were just losing game after game after game," Lackey says. "This is a book by a former drug addict about being a drug addict, and I'm identifying with it as a baseball fan. That can't be healthy."

Dry Land

Rooting for teams that represent particular regions feels natural to us as 21st-century Americans. But in the grand scheme of human existence, it isn't automatic that we would root for sports teams at all, let alone teams like the Pirates.

Psychologists Benjamin Winegard and Robert O. Deaner link sports fandom to traditional societies, where there would be evolutionary benefit in aligning oneself with a local group. In traditional societies, male mortality due to warfare might range from 13 percent to 30 percent, and so, Winegard and Deaner argue, local coalitions are vital for self-preservation. It is no accident, they say, that our most popular spectator sports involve men undertaking activities relevant to warfare, like running, tackling and throwing. Warfare also generally involves defending or attacking a particular geographical area, and sports fans ally themselves with teams from a particular geographical area. And victorious sports teams enjoy elevated social status – as in warfare, to the victors go the spoils.

Sports and warfare were even more intertwined centuries ago than they are today in warlike sports like mixed martial arts and football. In Rome, of course, gladiators fought wild animals, and each other, to the death. And for medieval knights, the line between sports and warfare was blurry indeed. As Allen Guttmann explains in his book *Sports Spectators*, "The warlike features of the tournament were especially pronounced in the twelfth century, when the typical tournament was a melee composed of parties of knights fighting simultaneously, capturing each other. ... Combats of this unregulated sort were apt to be deadly."

Winegard and Deaner point to a psychological concept called moral foundations theory, which attempts to explain the innate beginnings of humans' moral thought. There are five main categories of moral concerns: harm (whether an act helps or hurts), fairness, purity, authority (whether an act obeys, or respects, authority), and loyalty.

In males, sports fandom is strongly correlated with purity and respect for authority. In both sexes, though, sports fandom is most strongly connected to loyalty – if you're the sort of person who values loyalty very highly, rooting for a sports team is likely to appeal to you. That's lucky for the Pirates, obviously, since no other major American sports team has presented a tougher test of loyalty than the Bucs have.

The simplest explanation for why we root for sports teams, though, is that we want to define ourselves. "The brain really wants an answer to the who-am-I question," writes the journalist Eric Simons in his book *The Secret Lives of Sports Fans*, citing the sociologist Orrin Klapp. America's social structure once provided more decisive answers to that question, Simons suggests – we were workers, mothers, fathers, wives, husbands. We had strong ties to our hometowns and religious institutions. But in recent decades, as former societal pillars like good jobs and marriages and civic institutions began to crumble, we've tried to steady ourselves with sports fandom. Rooting for a sports team provides us with a sense of identity, which can fuel our self-esteem.

It isn't immediately obvious, though, how rooting for a sports team leads to self-esteem if that team doesn't win. Simons points to an area of psychology called social defeat, which scientists have studied by inducing physical confrontations between male rats. Researchers place a dominant rat in the same cage with a less powerful rat, which suffers a serious (but non-fatal) beating, which scientists consider an instance of social stress. (Think your cubicle job is stressful? Be grateful you're not a lab rat.)

The psychologist Kaj Björkqvist explains that, in social defeat experiments, the defeated rat is then subjected to *chronic* stress – it receives more beatings, or is housed near the dominant rat. The defeated rats undergo hormonal changes, including losses of testosterone and impaired immunological function. They lose interest in eating and sex. Defeated rats are also more likely to abuse drugs, more quickly turning to cocaine if it's made available to them. The defeated rat, in other words, becomes beaten down, not only physically, but psychologically. "It just becomes this horrible, sad-sack rat that loses all the time," Simons tells me.

Dry Land

The rats exhibit characteristics that researchers connect to depression in humans. Rats and humans both have a brain circuit called a reward system that releases dopamine when we experience something pleasurable, and defeated rats demonstrate decreased activity in their reward system.

Testing social defeat on humans is more difficult since, obviously, the tactics researchers use on rats would be illegal if used on people. But the idea is that the way rats respond to social defeat parallels the way humans respond to it. Simons, a die-hard Cal football fan, related to the idea of social defeat right away.

"I read this and I was like, 'Here's what happens to me when I watch Cal football!'" he says. "I think every fan out there in Pittsburgh and Cleveland and Buffalo is just reading this like, 'I'm that rat! That's me! They put me in a cage with the larger, aggressive, territorial asshole rat from wherever, and I lose.'"

In the past two decades, scientists have taken steps toward learning what happens in our brains when we watch sports. In the early 1990s, a group of neurophysicists in Italy led by Giacomo Rizzolatti wanted to know what neurons fired when a monkey prepared to eat a peanut. So they attached electrodes to the monkey's premotor cortex.

It worked. But the real discovery came later, when the researchers found that the neurons that fired when the monkey prepared to eat the peanut also fired when the monkey watched a human who was about to eat one. These are called mirror neurons, and humans have them too. The idea is that, when a fan watches Andrew McCutchen hit a baseball, mirror neurons fire as they would if the fan were *herself* the hitter.

"When you see me pull my arm back, as if to throw the ball, you also have in your brain a copy of what I am doing and it helps you understand my goal," Dr. Marco Iacoboni, a neurophysicist at UCLA, told the *New York Times* in 2006. "Because of mirror neurons, you can read my intentions. You know what I am going to do next.

"And if you see me choke up, in emotional distress from striking out at home plate, mirror neurons in your brain simulate my distress. You automatically have empathy for me. You know how I feel because you literally feel what I am feeling."

But when we're watching sports, mirror neurons don't work the same for everything we see. Instead, our brains help us use our mirror neurons so that we empathize more with our favorite teams than their opponents. Iacoboni thinks that mirror neurons are organized this way, at least in part, by our reward system.

"If you're a sports fan, you know that you may mirror Andrew McCutchen's joy, but you could watch someone else get hurt on another team and not care nearly as much, so you're not mirroring them as deeply," Simons tells me. "By deciding that you're a Pirates fan, you in some sense predetermine that your mirror neurons are not going to empathize with rival teams, [and] that you're going to empathize more deeply with your own team." When McCutchen hits a home run, we don't just *see* him do it. We *are* him.

What, then, should we expect of fans of a team that never has a winning season? Simons points to B.F. Skinner's midcentury experiments with operant conditioning. Skinner wanted animals to perform particular tasks, like raising their heads a certain way, and would give the animals food pellets once they did. After an animal learned that it could get a pellet by raising its head, though, Skinner began to experiment with *when* he dispensed the pellets. If the animal completely stopped receiving food pellets after raising its head, it would learn not to raise its head anymore. Which, of course, makes sense – the same principle, Skinner said, applies to humans. "If we lose a fountain pen, we reach less and less often into the pocket which formerly held it," he wrote.

But if the animal received a reward irregularly, it would continue to seek the reward for much longer than an animal that stopped receiving pellets entirely. An animal conditioned to receive intermittent rewards for performing a task might perform that task thousands more times after rewards had stopped.

Dry Land

So maybe if the Pirates never won, all fans, or almost all fans, would give up on the team. But they don't. Even in a bad year, the Bucs might win 60 of their 162 games, while teasing us with stretches where they play rather well. The Pirates effectively turn us into pigeons, raising our heads over and over in the hopes of receiving a bit of food. And then there's the problem of what, in sports fandom, constitutes a reward. Winning isn't the only food pellet we can receive. There's also the reward of watching a favorite player succeed, for example. But it's surely true that the fact that the Pirates continue winning at least occasionally helps keep us coming back, craning our necks over and over.

Another reason Pirates fans keep coming back is that our level of pleasure in a victory, or of pain in a loss, is calibrated by our expectation. During the streak, one would often hear Pirates fans say that the Bucs' decades of losing would make the next winning season that much sweeter. It turns out that's true, on a physiological level.

"[Y]our brain maps out a complex probability distribution for every reward it might get and then releases more or less dopamine depending on how predicted the reward was," Simons writes. In conversation with me later, he compares the brain to "a big bookie" – when your favorite team wins, your brain analyzes how likely that victory was. If your team wins a game you didn't expect it to, you'll feel more pleasure due to the dopamine surge, and if your team loses a game you expected it to lose, you'll feel less pain. So, in some sense, it isn't actually all that fun to be a fan of a team that wins all the time, like the Yankees. Being a Pirates fan is, obviously, worse, but when the Pirates finally win, it should feel amazing.

Daniel Wann, a psychology professor at Murray State University, studies the connections sports fans feel to their favorite teams. Dr. Wann's research deals with BIRGing, or Basking In Reflected Glory, and CORFing, which means Cutting Off Reflected Failure. Research shows that fans whose team is successful will tend to BIRG by, for example, wearing their team's apparel after a big win, or referring to their team as "we." Fans also CORF in response to losing teams, distancing themselves from losers as a way of managing blows to their egos. Hardcore fans appear to be less susceptible to BIRGing and CORFing than casual fans, and will maintain their associations with their teams through tough times.

But what will fans do when faced with a 20-year losing streak? Might hardcore fans be susceptible to CORFing in such an extreme circumstance?

"They get far more disgust and anguish and depression and frustration and violence out of the losing than the fair-weather fans do," Wann says. "It's just that being a fan of a team is so important to them [that] they're going to stick it out, with the hope that things will turn around, if not this year, then maybe next year."

Psychologically speaking, there's no reason to expect there to be any limits to their loyalty. In fact, Wann suggests, the losing might bond highly identified fans to their team even *more* strongly. He suggests turning the scenario around, and looking at a team that *wins* consistently.

"The Braves had that run of 13 straight years in the playoffs, and they would have a hard time selling out their playoff games," he says. "Because, in Atlanta, it got to the point of, 'Oh, well, we always make the playoffs. Wake me when the World Series rolls around.'" Serious Pirates fans will be grateful for what they can get, he suggests, and they won't give up on their team.

From an academic perspective, it's tough to generalize about the fan base of a major professional sports team, because any sports fan base consists of a relatively large and broad swath of a market's population. But Wann is a Royals fan, and he knows firsthand how constant losing can shape fans' approach to following their team.

"You can't really be a Pirates fans or a Royals fan ... without having developed ways of justifying why you're putting yourself through this misery year after year," he says. "So maybe if you're a fan of a long-suffering team, you've just perfected those strategies a bit."

Dry Land

Wann's research also deals with Cutting Off *Future* Failure, or COFFing. In one study, researchers organized small groups of undergraduate psychology students into "teams," ostensibly for the purpose of participating in a "creativity competition" against a group of artists. Some subjects were told they would participate in one round of competition, while others were told they would participate in two.

After the first round of the "competition" (which involved selecting the most creative shapes from renderings on sets of cards), study administrators told both the one-round and the two-round groups that, surprisingly, they had defeated the art students. Both groups were then asked whether they would be interested in meeting the art students they had just defeated. Subjects who were to participate in one round of competition proved to be more interested in meeting the art students than those who thought they would have to participate in another competition after winning the first one. That is, subjects who faced the prospect of losing in a second competition were more likely to COFF, protecting their egos in the face of a possible loss in the second competition, and, in the process, declining to "bask in the glow of their current success."

When I spoke to Dr. Wann in early September 2012, the Pirates still appeared to be headed for their first winning season in two decades, and I wondered how this research might affect Bucs fans if they did end up on the right side of .500. Might that cause some fans to COFF, and back away from the team?

Wann turned to his own experience with the Royals to answer that question. The Royals had a surprise winning season in 2003 after eight straight years of losing, and in 2004, their fans didn't back away. "That's not [the way] Royals fans thought," Wann says. "Spring Training 2004 could not [have arrived] quickly enough."

After a 7-14 April and a 10-17 May, though, it became clear that the 2004 Royals weren't going anywhere, and that's when the fans packed it in.

"There was so much optimism and so much hype, and then by June, you're like, 'Oh crap, here we go again,'" Wann says. The

56

Royals' attendance dropped from No. 10 in the American League in 2003 to No. 13, ahead of only the Devil Rays, in 2004. It then stayed at No. 13 until 2008, when it was dead last. So now that the Pirates' streak is over, the effect of their 2013 winning season might be brief, unless they can repeat it.

Still, Wann says, hope springs eternal. "The beauty of sports is that there really always is next year. And every year, in just about every sport, there's a team or two that has a season that makes you say, 'Well, hell, why can't that be us?'"

Simons tells me the "hope springs eternal" idea probably isn't enough on its own. Fortunately for the Pirates, though, plenty of reasons we follow the team (like our connections to the city of Pittsburgh and our family histories) have nothing to do with wins and losses, or the hope of more wins in the future. Simons also mentions that the Bucs could attract contrarian fans, an idea we'll explore later on.

Even though rooting for a baseball team is a choice, the experience of doing so can seem like it's controlling *us*, rather than the other way around. If you're a serious Pirates fan, you invested some percentage of your identity (hopefully not *too* great a percentage) in your team while it struggled for 20 straight years. As the team lost over and over, some part of you likely felt *yourself* losing. Over two decades, you may have sometimes felt like one of those defeated rats, cowering in the corner of a tiny box. The Pirates' losses were, in some sense, *your* losses. Seen from this perspective, the Pirates' 2013 season didn't just end the streak. It ended an entire nightmarish experiment. The streak is over. The scientists are done with you, little rat. You're free.

Chapter 4

Pirates fans' relationship with their team's history can be urgent, even desperate. For a team that gave its fans little to cheer for two decades, the past looms large, and not in the way it does for most fan bases.

Fans of all teams like to reminisce about past successes of their hometown boys, of course. But for Pirates fans, worship of the past is a deeper, and more pressing, phenomenon than it is elsewhere. The past is a life force, and one that became more diluted with each losing Pirates season. The fans cling to it, and so does the franchise, reminding us of the 1979 World Series team, in particular, at every opportunity.

This is partly because the sheer length of the baseball season provides plenty of opportunities for the team to promote its former players, and because of the existence of a cable channel (ROOT Sports) that serves mostly to broadcast Pirates and Penguins games and needs to fill time between matchups and during rain delays.

Pittsburgh also has a more vital connection with its past than many cities do, and so the past glories of its sports teams are more powerful for Pittsburgh fans than they possibly could be in, say, Columbus or Los Angeles. Bucs Dugout contributor David Manel points to "a sense of place" that one finds in old Pittsburgh neighborhoods like Squirrel Hill, or Bloomfield, with its cramped streets and slender row houses built into the hills. Because baseball is played every day, it's a part of the rhythm of everyday life in places like these, and its roots in the history of Pittsburgh *itself* are deep.

But it's also true that, at least during the streak, one reason the Pirates emphasized the history of their team is that fans *needed to be reminded* that good baseball once existed in Pittsburgh. Many older fans root for the Bucs due to their memories of the 1960s and 1970s, and especially the World Series teams of 1960, 1971 and 1979. The older fans were often the most bitter about the losing streak, perhaps understandably so, and they needed the past to believe there could be a future. The constant reminders of days gone by thus were not celebrations of the past in and of themselves, but rather a form of begging. *Please continue to pay attention,* they said. If the Pirates thought a Kent Tekulve tap-dance performance would have made a difference, I'm sure they would have had him do it.

20 years is a very long time, about a quarter of the time we get on this planet. A fan who was 65 in 2012 hadn't seen a winning season since age 45. If the streak had lasted another decade, that fan might not have gotten to see another winning season at all. This is one reason the streak seemed like such an urgent matter for older fans. Many of them thought of it in terms of *when they were going to die.* The significance of the streak transcended baseball. It was existential.

And the pain of the streak arguably stretched back earlier than 1993, when it officially began. The Pirates went 75-87 in 1984, and then were horrible the next two years, going 57-104 and 64-98 while embroiled in a cocaine scandal. From 1984 through 2012, the Pirates had a grand total of four winning seasons.

If a fan thought about the streak this way – the generation-spanning brutality of it – it was hard not to get upset. The only alternative was to simply let it go, and enjoy baseball for what it is: an afternoon or evening spent outdoors, in a beautiful ballpark, watching America's greatest game. This left the *Pirates* out of the equation, however – a fan who thought this way might as well have been watching the Idaho Falls Chukars, or the Long Island Ducks. Casual fans, the kind who viewed a Pirates game with a Skyblast display purely as a pleasant night out with the significant other or the family, mostly approached the Pirates during the streak as if they were some random minor-league team. Most hardcore fans found this line of thinking difficult to pull off, because it was tough to tune in each night without being invested in the outcome. But for some fans, it worked.

"Wins and losses don't affect my enjoyment of the game anymore," Mark Stacy, a fifty-something Bucs Dugout regular who lives in Morgantown, told me before the 2013 season.

"I don't need the frustration of getting worked up over a losing streak. I like sitting in the sun. I like the atmosphere in the ballpark. If we win the game, that's great. If we don't, it's not going to ruin my day," he says. "By this point, where else am I going to go? I'm not going to change allegiances or something like that. And so, for my own sanity, I just tell myself it's not that important to have a winning season, as long as there's baseball being played."

Older fans also sometimes compare the modern-day Pirates to winning Bucs teams from the past, which isn't always helpful, since the game simply has changed. "I've had a couple times where there's been people who ... are older, they tell me, 'You just don't understand what it's like. I've been there, so I know what this team can do,'" says Tim Williams of the website Pirates Prospects, pointing out that the disparities in salary between the richest and poorest teams make today's game totally different than it was decades ago.

Of course, a key motivator for many older fans is nostalgia.

Like most Pirates fans, Mary Jane Kuffner, who is about 60, traces her interest in the team back to elementary school. "Back then, if you had good grades, the Pirates would give you half a dozen tickets during the season," she says.

"The Pirates were part of your everyday life. It was in the days when your mother could drop you off at [the] field, and you could be by yourself, and she wouldn't have to worry. She'd just come back and pick you up when the game was over."

This isn't the first time I've heard a Pirates fan tell me almost exactly this. And when one thinks about baseball in these terms, it's easy to see why fans stick around. Baseball is a relic of a simpler, safer time, or at least that's how the thinking goes. Before cyber-stalking, before drones, and before AIDS, there was Pirates baseball. And if baseball's essence, to you, is a quiet game played in summer evenings at a ballpark where you and your fellow 11-year-olds could run around without your parents, you're probably unlikely to leave it behind, even if 11-year-olds can't run around by themselves anymore and the team doesn't win.

Beyond that, what keeps Kuffner coming back is loyalty. "Pittsburgh has a lot of fair-weather sports fans," she says. "That's inappropriate. If you're going to have a professional sports team in town, you have to support it."

I meet Mike, a 60-something retiree who's originally from New Kensington but now lives in the Cleveland area, as we're both leaning on the railing of the PNC Park rotunda, watching the Pirates play the Chicago Cubs. It's a great day for baseball (well, until a fourth-inning rain delay, but that's par for the course for Pittsburgh in May), and we experience an odd sort of dislocation as we talk about 20 years of losing while watching the Pirates jump out to an early lead. Mike says he reacts to the Pirates' long losing streak in about the same way he reacts to negative reports that appear in the news more generally.

"You just watch the news, and you try to deal with *that* shit," Mike says. "The news tops itself every day."

Mike finds the Pirates' losing tough to square with what he saw in the 1960s and 1970s. "It's hard for me to believe this team that was so good has the record for most losing seasons," he says.

Like many older Pirates fans, Mike sees the Bucs' losing as merely part of a series of changes that have made the game less accessible to fans like him. For example, he cites the fact that players change teams more frequently now than they did a generation ago.

"They move around so much," Mike says. "Back in the old days, I knew the lineups."

Nonetheless, Mike keeps following the game, albeit with a bit of ironic distance. "To stay interested, you sort of look at it as a joke. It's comedy," he says.

That helps him stay at peace with all the losing, as he looks back fondly at the great baseball he saw in the old days.

"I can take solace in knowing that the Bill Mazeroski [home run] will always be in our minds, in Pittsburgh's mind."

I was born the same week the Pirates won their last World Series, in 1979, and I was still only three at the end of the 1983 season, when the Bucs finished 84-78 for the second year in a row before the start of five straight losing seasons. But I still got to see four winning teams – 1988, and 1990-1992 – before the Pirates vanished into the thin air of the Clinton years. And the brief time in my life when the Pirates were good was a formative time for a young baseball fan, an age where the blossoming baseball geek devours every statistic he finds on the backs of his trading cards. When the losing streak began, in 1993, I was 13. The die had already been cast.

But what about for younger Pirates fans, fans who, before 2013, hadn't seen a winning season *in their entire lives*? What motivated them to stick with the team?

It's not as if the Pirates didn't do *anything* worthy of fans' attention in the previous two decades. Jason Kendall, Brian Giles, Jason Bay and Andrew McCutchen did provide the Pirates with genuine stars. And, of course, there was PNC Park. Younger fans didn't get to see great baseball, but they *did* get to watch baseball in the greatest place. The Pirates have played in PNC for less than two decades, and yet the park already occupies a special place in the city's heart. PNC isn't just beautifully built, but beautifully positioned, overlooking downtown Pittsburgh and, crucially, the Roberto Clemente Bridge, which not only provides a path to walk to the ballpark, but a reminder to fans *in* the ballpark that they're *in Pittsburgh*, a city built around rivers, and a city that gets its signature look from bridges like this one. While the younger fans didn't have even one winning season on which to hang their caps, they did, at least, grow up with PNC Park as their home base.

Some younger fans, such as Bucs Dugout commenter Battling-Bucs, point to the 1997 Freak Show team, which stayed in contention until fall despite a tiny payroll and a lack of superstar talent, as a reason they developed an interest in the Pirates. "The Steelers and, to a smaller extent, the Penguins came within my family, but my dedication to the Pirates came from me alone," he writes. "I remember the brooms in the stands for the nine-million-dollar team versus the ten-million-dollar-man [Chicago White Sox slugger Albert Belle], and the Francisco Cordova / Ricardo Rincon no-hitter, with [the] Mark Smith walk-off home run."

Near the beginning of the following season, Pirates veteran Turner Ward, manning right field in Three Rivers Stadium in a game against the Dodgers, went back on a line drive off the bat of Mike Piazza. Ward made the catch right before slamming his upper body into the outfield wall. One of its blue panels sprang open awkwardly, and Ward tumbled behind the wall and briefly disappeared from view before jumping up, tossing the ball toward the infield and grabbing his shoulder.

The Pirates teams that played during the streak weren't especially talented. But they had a few things going for them. If absolutely everything broke right, they might contend, or at least sniff .500, for a few months. And when they didn't, the basic equilibrium of baseball kept them from being *too* terrible. It's hard to lose more than 100 games in a season, and during the streak, the Pirates only managed to do it once. So on any given day, they'd have about a 40 percent chance of winning. And if you caught them at just the right time, they might just run through a wall for you.

But is that enough? Are the limited charms of rooting for an awful team in a great stadium, along with whatever meaning one might wring out of one's local and family connections to the franchise, enough to sustain a fan who's never even seen his team finish .500?

Greg Allison, a 21-year-old fan who spent 2012 making a documentary about the season, rooted for the Atlanta Braves as a teenager but turned to the Pirates after enrolling in college in Pittsburgh. He describes his conversion almost as an intellectual problem to be solved.

"It seemed interesting, just because Pirates fans, because the team has been so bad, we almost try to put ourselves in the role of GM," he says. "So, in a way, it was me kind of thinking, 'Alright, well, maybe I can learn about this team, and I'll be the one to fix whatever problems they're having.'"

The fact that what's best for the Pirates isn't always obvious, even when they do things right, interested Allison. "It got me curious, because from a distance, when you don't know things, it just seems like everything they do is stupid. Like when they traded [outfielder Nate] McLouth, it made me more of a fan, because everybody was saying, 'Oh, that's so stupid, they traded their best player.' I had to feel like there was something more behind it."

This was a motivating factor for me, too. I'm fundamentally more attracted to baseball than to other sports. But there's also the fact that as a Pittsburgh sports fan, if the Steelers, for example, make a move that doesn't appear to make sense, you can usually assume there's a good reason for it that isn't yet clear to you. In fact, that's what most Steelers fans do, or at least what they did prior to 2012 or so.

On the other hand, if the *Pirates* make a move that doesn't provide an obvious, immediate upgrade, the default assumption is that they did it because they're cheap, or stupid. I returned to the Pirates at the end of the Cam Bonifay years and in the Dave Littlefield years, when the Pirates typically *were* being cheap and/or stupid, but I still felt a perverse thrill upon discovering that was, in fact, true, and in many cases was even worse than it seemed.

It helped that baseball, which is based around one-against-one battles between batters and pitchers, led so smoothly to that sense of discovery. In baseball, it's easier to wring meaning from statistics, even minor-league statistics, than it is in other team sports. "With the Pirates, you can scrutinize every Rule 5 pick," Allison says. "In a way, baseball's better because people tend to have more of a track record."

It isn't new for fans to be interested in armchair general managing, of course, but it's no accident that Allison's approach to the Pirates is most common among younger fans, who have grown up making fantasy baseball trades and playing baseball video games in franchise mode. A few of them take this style of fandom to amazing extremes.

"I don't really care if the team wins or not," Connor Jennings, 21, told me before the 2013 season. "Them winning is interesting, and I like to see them be successful, but I prefer to watch individual players.

"I would rather be Organization of the Year than win the World Series," he says, referring to the *Baseball America* award for the franchise with the best package of team, general manager, manager and minor-league talent. "If the team starts being competitive now, I'll be the kind of person [who] wants to trade Andrew McCutchen for an exciting package of prospects."

Pittsburgh media types and older Pirates fans sometimes accuse younger fans of thinking this way. Most genuinely don't, and of course it's possible to be deeply invested in the process of rebuilding a franchise while appreciating that the process needs to serve some broader purpose. But there *are* a few fans whose interest in rebuilding is an end in itself.

Is that sabermetrics, or fantasy baseball, run amok? Probably. But it's also probably a coping mechanism. Before the streak, younger Pirates fans knew, intellectually, that the Bucs probably wouldn't lose forever. But I doubt they really *felt* that, or appreciated it, because they never knew the team when it was a winner.

"I like baseball, the business, probably more than baseball, the sport," Jennings says.

And why not? Baseball, the business, *is* interesting. And becoming a serious Pirates fan during the first few Neal Huntington years must have been *very* interesting, because while the mainstream perception of the Pirates' motivations didn't change, the Pirates' *actual* motivations did, as they sensibly began focusing on the draft and Latin America. But in some quarters, fans' outlooks on the Pirates became *more* pessimistic, because part of Huntington's plan was trading popular major-league players – like McLouth, Jack Wilson and Jason Bay – for prospects. For Greg Allison, part of the appeal of following the Pirates involved breaking from the conventional wisdom.

Then there's identifying with the Pirates *precisely because they're unpopular*. For Brian McElhinny, a 21-year-old fan who runs the Pirates blog Raise The Jolly Roger, becoming a Pirates fan was, in part, a way of distinguishing himself – *from his peers in South Hills*, where you might think rooting for the Pirates would be about as useful a distinguishing feature for a young man as hating one's parents, or wanting to bang Kate Upton.

"Liking the Pirates kind of just became my *thing*," McElhinny told me in 2012. "You're not jumping on the bandwagon. Being an intense Pirates fan is pretty unique, I think."

It's worth stopping for a second to let that sink in: For McElhinny, the Pirates were a small enough cultural niche *even in suburban Pittsburgh* that his interest in them helped him distinguish himself from his peers, in about the same way an interest in goth music or skateboarding might. That speaks to how little the Pirates mattered to most young Pittsburghers during the streak. At least among young people, the Pirates were on the fringes of mainstream culture, even in the Pittsburgh area.

David Manel is in his early forties, but he became a Pirates fan in the midst of the streak. He grew up rooting for the Detroit Tigers, but started pulling for the Bucs when he arrived in Pittsburgh in 1997. Before that, he grew up rooting for Michigan State over the University of Michigan and wearing Spartans gear at Halloween, both in an era in which Michigan's major sports teams were much more successful than those of Michigan State.

Dry Land

"There's something about that kind of fandom that's really attractive," he says. "Watching a team build. Watching the improvement.

"That's why it was really easy, when I moved from Detroit to here, to adopt the Pirates immediately. If I had moved to Boston, or New York ... there's something more romantic [about following the Pirates]."

That's probably true. My own efforts to follow the Red Sox, and the Padres, ultimately failed. But perhaps that was partly because *those teams were good.* (The Padres won 87 games the year I arrived in San Diego, and two division titles in the years after that.) Simply switching from a losing team to a winning one isn't very sporting. If I'd moved to Tampa in 2006, as the Rays were losing but putting together the pieces of a contender, that might have been different.

In any case, Pirates fans not old enough to recall a winning season were often forced to become fans of the game in general.

"I think all the losing made me a better fan," writes a Bucs Dugout commenter. "Since I started following in '92 (lucky me), all the losing meant I had to become a fan of the *game*, not just of winning, or of my favorite team."

For Pirates fans during the streak, the holy grail was a winning season, just one year above .500. Pirates fans over the age of 28 or so at least had some clue about how they would react when it happened. The younger ones didn't.

"The crazy thing is, I don't even know," McElhinny said. "When the Steelers won the Super Bowl, I was very happy. When the Penguins won the Stanley Cup, I was happy. ... You know, party, whatever. I can guarantee that it's nothing like it would be like if the Pirates were to be even in the playoffs."

26-year-old Sarah Fleck, who's originally from Johnstown but now lives in California, has no direct memories of the last winning Pirates season before 2013 and lost track of the Pirates through her teens, but became a serious fan beginning in 2004, in the midst of the dismal Littlefield years. She left for college, and reconnected

Charlie Wilmoth

with baseball – and with the Pirates – through a friend whose relationship with the Pirates she describes as "really sad."

"[I was] like, 'Why do you put yourself through this all the time?'" she says.

And yet *she* ended up stuck with the Pirates too. "I have this fierce loyalty to Western Pennsylvania and Pittsburgh, so when I realized I liked baseball, it was like, 'Duh, I'm going to be a Pirates fan,'" she laughs. "It was like an underdog complex, maybe. I liked them for their dysfunctionality."

Generally, younger fans seem happier about the Pirates than older fans do. Since, before 2013, they had never seen their team win, they didn't know what it felt like, unless they had some point of reference from other sports. They had also grown up with PNC Park as their home base, and they tended to see attending a Pirates game as a pleasant experience, even if the Bucs lost. That didn't make younger fans any less serious than older ones. But it meant the losing bothered the younger generation less.

"I may have never seen them have a winning season, but they still win a lot of games every year," 24-year-old season-ticket holder Christy Rosati told me during summer 2013. "Never really knowing what it's like to have a winning season, to me it's still, 'Hey, they might win this game,' and that's the game I care about at the time." Besides, she notes, even a great baseball team will lose about 60 times a year. She compares baseball to following football or hockey. "[With] the sheer quantity of games, you're going to lose more," she says. "You have to handle it better."

Rosati is used to watching games without worrying too much about their context. She goes to games, she roots, and she doesn't worry much about the standings (although she jokes that the Pirates have a good record in games she attends). When I spoke to her in July 2013, she was excited to watch a team that had a good shot at the playoffs, noting that she enjoyed the 2012 season even after the team fell apart, because it was still technically in the playoff race late into the year. "Last season was the first time I went to a meaningful baseball game in September," she says.

Dry Land

Ultimately, part of her happiness with the team has to do with the fact that she simply doesn't have much experience rooting for a winning team. (She's a fan of the Steelers and Penguins, but doesn't follow them nearly as closely.) But it's also that she simply doesn't take the results too personally. "I really enjoy the game, and I take it for entertainment," she says. "My life's not going to be ruined if the Pirates lose."

93.7 The Fan host Colin Dunlap, who is in his late 30s, identifies a "purgatory" between the two groups, into which falls a generation of fans that remembers the last winning team, but doesn't remember the last world championship.

"I saw a team that was probably good enough, but didn't get there," Dunlap says, referring to the Pirates of the early 1990s.

"There was no way in the world that you could wrap your head around fast-forwarding 20 years and saying, 'They're not even going to win more games than lose in a season,'" he says. "For somebody who is an eighth-grader, going through that, you're like, 'Man, this is a great baseball town,' and then there was a drop-off point. It was precipitous."

Dunlap says the Pirates' decline, which occurred in his formative teenage years, hardened him, and his limited experience with good teams gave him little to lean on. "You get called a cynic or whatever," he says. "I don't have that [connection to] the romanticism of Clemente and Mazeroski and those old-timers. I can't romanticize how great Forbes Field was."

At the same time, he says, "I don't have the PNC Park experience of, 'I'm a young person and I love fireworks and bobblehead dolls, and that's why I go to games,' because I remember when they were good."

If older Pirates fans belong to Forbes Field and younger ones to PNC Park, then, fans who are currently about 30 to 40 belong to the sad concrete circle of Three Rivers Stadium, where they saw three playoff runs and little else. The streak unfolded while they went to high school, and then college, and then got their first jobs, and per-

70

haps had children. They knew what rooting for a winning team was like, but they didn't have the experience of winning it all.

Before the 2012 season, the Pirates tweeted a photo of former Bucs catcher Mike LaValliere and second baseman Jose Lind dressed in Pirates uniforms and clowning around at Pirates Fantasy Camp. LaValliere carried Lind over his shoulder, with Lind tilting head-first, as if about to fall to the Florida grass. It had been almost 20 years since the two men had played together, and they still essentially looked the way we remembered them – LaValliere barrel-chested and mustachioed, Lind small and wiry. Now, though, they both sported gray facial hair. LaValliere's meaty hand grasped Lind's wrist, and their arms met near LaValliere's wristwatch, which ticked away the passage of time. It probably didn't read "20 years," but it could have. The members of the Pirates' last playoff team were now middle-aged, and their heroics were now in the distant past. Pirates fans had changed along with them.

Chapter 5

"I'm done with this team."

Pirates fans have heard these five words many times. After nearly every disappointment, a blog commenter, message-board poster or Twitter user will declare that this time, the misdeeds of the Pirates' ownership and front office have become too much, and this fan is ready to take his or her enthusiasm elsewhere. Pirates fall apart down the stretch? *I'm done with this team!* Eric Hinske batting cleanup? *I'm done with this team!* Pretzel at PNC Park have too much salt? *I'm! Done! With!* ... Well, you get the idea.

These threats wouldn't be so silly if the fans who made them had any track record of following through. The Pirates lost for 20 years running, so quitting on the team during that period, and spending the effort and money on something else, frankly would have made a lot of sense. *I* couldn't do it, but there certainly would have been logic to it.

Most of those who threatened to quit never did, however. Perhaps some fans felt quitting made sense, but they didn't have the wherewithal to go through with it. In any case, tracking who, exactly, quits on the team, and for how long, is difficult, because so many threats turn out to be empty.

Late one night in October 2012, I put up a thread on Bucs Dugout requesting information on fans (relatives and friends of Bucs Dugout readers, perhaps) who had given up. When I woke, I had one blog comment (which said that real fans don't give up on their teams) and two emails, both from gentlemen who claimed that, despite apparently noticing a headline minutes after it was posted in the middle of the night in the fourth spot of a Pirates blog, *they themselves* had renounced their Pirates fandom.

"I can give you three reasons why I did so. [Assistant general manager] Kyle Stark, Neal Huntington, and Frank Coonelly," wrote one. "The arrogance of the front office in the face of the disturbing revelations of the [Navy SEAL] training, Hells Angels, and the dismissive way they treated former players looking to help the team have soured me on further support."

"I had hope when Bob Nutting said he was essentially going to get the bottom of things. I expected heads to roll," wrote the other. "A few days later, Coonelly crushed my hopes of that happening. I could see that essentially another year of no changes was on the way and that, to me, was it."

The Pirates' use of Navy SEAL training had become news less than two weeks earlier, and a bizarre, but harmless, email from Stark involving a simile about the Hells Angels had been leaked to the media. Presumably in response to mounting criticism and speculation over the Pirates' late-season collapse, Coonelly had announced a few days later that the jobs of Huntington, Stark and fellow assistant GM Greg Smith were safe.

In other words, these two readers were reacting to news that had broken two weeks before, in the wake of the team's epic 2012 collapse. They would be back.

More responses trickled in. One fan told me she had attended 40 games in 2011 and more than 30 in 2012, but that she was "tired of sitting at lousy games in September" and was considering switching allegiances to the Phillies, the team she rooted for growing up. But when spring training started, she said, "Maybe I'll feel different."

"Every year I threaten to find another team to root for, but I always come back," another fan wrote. "My own stupidity, I guess."

Finally, after about two days, I found a serious Pirates fan who quit because their situation simply got to be too much. Dave Sutor, a 39-year-old reporter from Johnstown, went to his first Pirates game in 1980. The Pirates' World Series championship in 1979 is among his earliest sports memories. He followed the team for two decades, but gave up when the Bucs traded Aramis Ramirez in 2003.

"[It] wasn't worth investing emotionally in watching them play," he says. "It just seemed like the whole process was going through the motions, and the winning didn't seem to matter anymore."

Even before the Ramirez trade, he says, he had begun to feel like he was rooting for the Pirates out of obligation, rather than desire.

"The connection was broken for me," he says. "This just happens to be a team that's playing baseball, and they happen to be geographically closest to me. It's not the same organization that I grew up watching."

He drifted away from the game almost entirely, unable to muster the enthusiasm to follow another team. He now goes to one game at PNC Park every year, usually to an interleague game to watch a team he hasn't seen before. Other than that, he stays away.

Of course, some fans do give up and leave. Others give up (or return) for reasons that don't have much to do with the Pirates' won-loss record. For example, one fan told me that he had recently moved to Philadelphia and wondered whether he should switch his rooting interest so that his young son could grow up as a Phillies fan. Another said he gave up on the Pirates (and baseball) during the players' strike in 1981, and returned to both in 2012.

It may also be that fans who give up on the team completely aren't easy to find because they weren't particularly serious fans to begin with. A fan's abandonment of a team is probably less like an avalanche and more like a few pebbles rolling a few feet downhill every so often. The serious fan, fed up with decades of losing, does not disappear completely, but merely becomes a slightly less serious fan. It's the fair-weather fan who is more likely to vanish.

Dry Land

In general, though, fans probably don't quit on the team nearly as much as they claim. The Bucs drew 2,091,918 fans in 2012; in their last winning season before that, 1992, they drew 1,829,395. The 1979 World Series team drew 1,435,454. There are, of course, any number of reasons for those disparities, one of them being that PNC Park is a much nicer place to watch a game than Three Rivers Stadium was. But Pittsburgh's population has dropped precipitously since about 1960, and the population of its metro area has also fallen. Fans are more apt to support winning teams, but that's always been the case – the 1985 Pirates, who won 57 games, drew a paltry 735,900 fans. When the Pirates finally began winning, in 2013, the crowds were enormous.

The Pirates are, if nothing else, a fascinating case study in fan loyalty. Take away PNC Park, and it would be hard to imagine better conditions in which to study it. With most teams, after one becomes a fan, it's relatively easy to remain one. Sports teams may disappoint us, sometimes bitterly, but there's always next year. A fan's enthusiasm might wax and wane, but even in tough times, the possibility of a better future makes it easy to keep going.

For much of the Pirates' streak, though, that better future was difficult to see. Even in the Huntington years leading up to 2013, there were interesting minor-leaguers, and Bucs fans followed them closely, but usually without truly believing those prospects would make much of a difference. Bucs fans, still gun-shy about their earlier enthusiasms for busts like Chad Hermansen, Bryan Bullington, and Jimmy Anderson, had a hard time trusting their team's talent until they saw it on display in the majors. And even if most Pirates fans believed, intellectually, that the Bucs' young players would one day put them over the top, believing it *emotionally* was a difficult hurdle to clear.

While doing interviews for this book, I did talk to a few Pirates fans whose love for the team seemed unaffected by Pirates' decades of struggle. I must admit that I didn't really understand how, after 20 years, a fan could express nothing but bland optimism about the Bucs, and in most cases, I also couldn't figure out how to penetrate that optimism to see what lay beneath it. For some fans, it's probably simply a case of staying loyal to one's home team, and not wanting to say anything bad about the team when things aren't going so well.

These kinds of fans are in the minority, however. To be a Pirates fan is to struggle. To *stop* being one is a struggle. I'm not sure which struggle is more radical. But many Pirates fans seem to be involved in both struggles at the same time.

One manifestation of those struggles entered the news in 2007, when local businessman Andy Chomos led a group called Pirates Fans for Change in protest at PNC Park. "I think, like everybody, my passion for Pirates baseball has been beaten down by so many years of losing," Chomos told Pittsburgh *CityPaper*. "I'm about as optimistic a person as you're going to find, and even the eternal optimist eventually gets to the point where you're discouraged."

In late June, Chomos addressed the media near the Roberto Clemente statue outside the center field gate at PNC. "Don't let this bobblehead replace the legacy that man created," said Chomos, holding up a Ronny Paulino doll. "Bobbleheads, blankets, trinkets. … We all have enough crap in our house." Chomos organized a walkout during a game in PNC Park.

Fans had plenty of reasons for their anger, stretching back at least to the 2003 Ramirez deal. "They had a lot of bad players, and dumpster-diving every year," says Pirates fan Steve Zielinski. "There was [an] amassing of opposition to the team. A lot of people jumped on that bandwagon really quickly."

In 2006, Zielinski created a website called Irate Fans – the logo featured a "P" falling away from the word "Pirate" – that briefly was a megaphone for fan discontent. I and several other writers contributed essays to the site; mine generally focused on Dave Littlefield's incompetence. But the website didn't really go anywhere on its own, and Zielinski expected it would run its course after the 2006 season.

Dry Land

In 2007, however, Littlefield's decision to draft Danny Moskos instead of Matt Wieters lit a fire under the fan base in a way that the previous season hadn't. With the fourth overall pick in the draft, the Pirates had selected a lefty who projected as a reliever instead of a potentially franchise-changing star catcher. Littlefield's exact motivations, whether they were financial or baseball-related, were unclear, but what *was* clear was that the Pirates' general manager wasn't acting in the organization's best interest.

Chomos quickly emerged as a leader of what might or might not have been called a movement. Chomos' group mostly existed separately from what Irate Fans was doing.

"He was actually unaware of the Irate Fans [website]," Zielinski says. "He just got pissed off. Everything just kind of jelled around him."

Chomos says he received encouragement from *Post-Gazette* writer Bob Smizik, who told Chomos he would support a protest as long as it did not affect the jobs of PNC Park workers. That led to support from other quarters of the Pittsburgh media.

In late June, Fans for Change made its biggest statement, with its members dressing in green shirts and walking out in the third inning of a game against the Nationals. Before the game, fans met outside a sports bar near PNC Park, where former Bucs star Dock Ellis addressed them.

"I've sort of been embarrassed to be called a Pirate over the last 15 years, and that hurts," said Ellis, according to the *Post-Gazette*'s Robert Dvorchak. "You have to give the fans something. They deserve something. Let's hope that management takes notice."

In response to growing publicity for the protest, Bob Nutting – who had only recently supplanted Kevin McClatchy as the public face of Pirates ownership – issued a statement. He also appeared on a game telecast that weekend. "Frankly, we all share in the frustration," he said.

The protest itself was uninspiring. After the third inning, a slow trickle of fans made their way to the exits. Confusion over when they were supposed to leave was a factor, but the main problem was that the protesters represented a small percentage of the crowd to begin with.

"Nobody really cares," says Wilbur Miller. "The vast majority of the fans in the ballpark really don't follow the team that closely, and they just look at it like people in this culture generally look at anybody who's protesting something. They just think they're weirdos."

"The mistake that we made is we should have told everybody to go to a common [gathering] point after the third inning," Chomos tells me. "There was confusion about what inning people should get up. I saw after the second inning, I saw about a thousand people getting up, running to the foyers with green shirts on, and I'm like, 'Oh shit, there's the first communication gaffe.'" Had Twitter been popular at the time, Chomos notes, there wouldn't have been such confusion.

"And then after the third inning, when the other, say, two thousand, three thousand people that actually had the guts to walk off did it, there was a chorus of boos from the rest of the people that opted to stay in their seats," Chomos continues. "Largely, a lot of the people were booing because the Pirates were winning 6-1 at the time."

Some fans also disagreed with Fans for Change's tactics, particularly the organization's decision to hold the protest *inside* the stadium, which meant that you had to buy a ticket to participate. Because the protest involved giving the Pirates money, some fans figured the Bucs' ownership would be laughing all the way to the bank.

"If we would've tried to do something outside the stadium, I guarantee I could've worked at it for a year, and maybe got 50 people to try to sit in on the Sixth Street Bridge," Chomos says, adding that part of the protest's point was to include season-ticket holders, who would be inside the park anyway.

The ultimate impact of the protest remains unclear. But a week later, Kevin McClatchy stepped down as the Pirates' CEO.

Dry Land

"I take responsibility for the losing, that's probably in some ways reason for a change," McClatchy told the Associated Press.

McClatchy wasn't the only departure of that period. Weeks later, Littlefield made his ridiculous trade for Matt Morris, and, amid escalating criticism, Nutting fired Littlefield. (There's a conspiracy theory about the Morris deal that Littlefield knew he would be fired, and took on Morris' salary as a way of sticking it to Nutting. I see it more as a Hail-Mary attempt to be competitive the rest of the season, but it shows how hazy the line between evil and stupid can be.)

Nutting then hired Coonelly and Huntington. Fans were, of course, slow to see those two as an improvement, and they were hardly perfect. But Nutting also committed large sums to the draft until MLB's rules changed following the 2011 season, and the organization underwent a much-needed rebuild that elevated it above abject hopelessness. Perhaps the protest had nothing to do with these changes. Actually, it probably didn't. But the protesters got much of what they wanted, and it led to crucial improvements to the organization.

Chapter 6

A prolonged losing streak will tend to breed extremist fans. Until 2013, Bucs fans were exactly that. Many either thought they knew how to fix the Pirates, or were outraged that, in their estimation, the Pirates didn't seem to want to fix themselves. Or both.

Extremist sports fans exist everywhere. "Fan" is short for "fanatic," after all. But the Pirates' situation created tons of wild-eyed anger, and the losing streak went on for so long that it became a crucial part of who Pirates fans were.

No one knows the really extreme Pirates fans better than the 93.7 The Fan radio personality Chris Mueller, who moved into drive time after the 2012 season but previously worked the late-night shift, where he trolled the Pirates' least reasonable fans – in the middle of the night, at their least reasonable moments – with almost religious fervor.

"When you have 19 straight losing seasons, it creates bunker mentalities," Mueller told me in 2012. If a team typically wins an average or above-average number of games, its fan base will generally be harmonious, as is mostly the case with the Steelers and Penguins. If not, well …

Since 2008 or so, the crucial axis dividing Pirates fans has been that of the Bucs ownership and front office. This is truer on the internet than in real life, and was truer until about August 2013 than it is today. Still, the best way to get Pirates fans arguing is to mention

Dry Land

Bob Nutting, Frank Coonelly or Neal Huntington. This is, obviously, not a phenomenon entirely unique to fans of the Pirates – plenty of owners and general managers are lightning rods. What's unique about Pirates fans' feelings about Nutting, Coonelly and Huntington is their intensity, particularly on the negative side.

Builders

A large subspecies of fans that are perceived to be pro-management or pro-front office consists of what Mueller calls "realistic types." Here, we'll call them "Builders." These fans are typically sabermetrically-inclined, and tend to see the Pirates' situation in terms of hard truths about baseball in small markets. The Tampa Bay Rays – who organize their team around young players, make shrewd trades, tend not to pay heavily for veterans, and generally pursue a rigidly rational approach – represent the Builder's ideal of how the Pirates should be run. Builders argue that "you have to be at the forefront, you have to be ahead of everybody else," Mueller says. "They get that you need to [stockpile] arms in the minor leagues, and that you need to have a couple kids break out. ... They get that there's luck in it, and there's ways to go about [doing] certain things."

The Builder, in other words, understands the importance of the Pirates' farm system and appreciates the amount of time it takes to turn a moribund franchise around. The Builder tends to make his or her home on Pirates blogs (either on the front page or the comments section), or on Twitter.

The Builder tries to view his or her team in a dispassionate light. That's not easy, and maybe it *shouldn't* be easy. The Builder preached patience with Neal Huntington and Bob Nutting, but it was difficult to have that patience while the losing streak wore on for two decades. The Pirates' losing streak was not only unsatisfying, but embarrassing. Patience might be the best way out of an embarrassing situation, but that doesn't make it easy to practice, especially if your team is losing and you feel your city's reputation is on the line.

The blogger Tim Williams, in comparing his outlook on the Pirates to that of the *Tribune-Review* columnist Dejan Kovacevic, explains that he tends to be more patient, in part, because he doesn't tie the team's fortunes to city pride.

"I write about Pittsburgh, but I don't care a lot about Pittsburgh," says Williams, who follows Pittsburgh teams due to family connections but grew up elsewhere. "Taken out of context, that could be bad. But I think Dejan looks at it as, he has a lot of pride in the city. ... So I think he takes it a little more [personally] if a Pittsburgh team isn't doing well."

Of course, most Pirates fans, Builders included, *do* care a lot about Pittsburgh. If they didn't, most of them would root for other teams. But it's no accident that Builders, in their less tolerant moments, sometimes describe those who disagree with them as "yinzers," a slur (at least in this context; it can also be a term of endearment) that refers to participants in Pittsburgh culture.

It's also no surprise that Builderism tends to thrive on the internet. The internet favors logical, premise-by-premise arguments more than the barstool or the bleachers do, for one thing. But the internet also allows far-flung fans to communicate, and many Builders watch the Pirates from afar. They're fans of the city of Pittsburgh, but they're also fans of *baseball*, and the latter may, in some cases, be more important to them. And so they have an easier time appreciating that, for example, assembling the core of a contender takes time, and that the Pirates might have little choice but to put up with a bad team in the short term. A team that is bad in the present does not seem quite as depressing to the Builder as it might be to other fans, because the Builder often has some geographical and social distance from the day-to-day reality of losing.

Some of the highest-profile Pirates blogger types (David Todd, David Manel and Vlad from Bucs Dugout, for example) live in Pittsburgh. But, for example, Williams has run Pirates Prospects

Dry Land

from Virginia and Florida, and Pat Lackey started WHYGAVS as a Duquesne student but has lived in North Carolina for several years.

"I'm not part of the media echo chamber in the city," says Ed Giles, a Meadville resident who grew up in Columbus, and who now runs the popular @InClementeWthr Twitter account.

"The performance of the sports teams is a large part of the identity, particularly for men, in the city," Giles says. "When one of those teams is letting them down, they almost take it as a personal slight, like, 'Neal Huntington doesn't care about me.' Well, I should *hope* that Neal Huntington doesn't care about you, because you have no real relationship to how his job goes.

"There's this expectation that the sports teams will have a sense of duty to the local population to preserve this idea of Pittsburgh being the city of champions," Giles continues. "Growing up in Columbus and living other places, I just didn't have to hear stuff like that regularly. I think when you live in the city, there's a certain amount of yourself that is affected by how well the sports teams are doing, beyond just being a fan of those teams."

Another reason the Builder might find rebuilding to be less painful is that he or she appreciates rebuilding as a process. The Builder finds losing without purpose – the kind of losing the Pirates did under Dave Littlefield – to be unwatchable. But losing *with* purpose, the way the Pirates did for their first few years under Huntington, is interesting. Not ideal, obviously. But interesting. Losing baseball goes down more easily if you appreciate what the franchise is trying to do.

The last six years represent the first time since Giles began paying attention that the Pirates have really rebuilt, and Giles says he enjoyed watching the Bucs change after Huntington took over in 2007. Around that time, Giles says, "I had become more familiar with the analytical side of baseball. It was more exciting to me. And that's what inspired me to start thinking more about [baseball] and following along more closely."

Upon being hired, Huntington found the franchise in disarray. In the NFL, it's possible to turn a losing franchise into a winning one rather quickly – drafting a franchise quarterback can make a huge difference all by itself. But it was likely to take at least four or five years to turn the Pirates around. There wasn't much hope for the Pirates to buy their way out of last place. They didn't have the money, for one thing, and the track record of teams that try to paper over massively flawed franchises with expensive free agents is sketchy at best. So the Bucs had little choice but to build through their farm system, and that takes time, particularly if there isn't much of a farm system there to begin with.

Following the 2007 season, the Pirates fired Jim Tracy, who had not endeared himself to Pirates fans – he took to the press to blame players for the Bucs' struggles, and boastfully compared the Pirates' situation to those of the Dodgers teams he had managed. The Bucs replaced him with John Russell, who was almost a complete nonentity as a leader, although he wasn't nearly as obnoxious as Tracy had been.

Other than that, Huntington's first offseason went quietly. He sent reliever Salomon Torres to the Brewers, took Evan Meek in the Rule 5 Draft, made a series of waiver claims, and signed infielder Chris Gomez and pitcher Byung-Hyun Kim. None qualified as major moves, and it appeared that Huntington wanted to give Littlefield's Bucs one last shot to compete.

Unsurprisingly, that didn't work. By July 2008, the Pirates were ten games below .500. So Huntington began dismantling the team. He started by sending outfielder Xavier Nady and reliever Damaso Marte to the Yankees for outfielder Jose Tabata and pitchers Jeff Karstens, Ross Ohlendorf and Daniel McCutchen. Then, he shipped Jason Bay to the Red Sox in a three-team trade, receiving third baseman Andy LaRoche, outfielder Brandon Moss and pitchers Bryan Morris and Craig Hansen in return. (Andy LaRoche played across the Pirates' infield from his brother, and fans dubbed Adam "Mario" and younger brother Andy "Luigi.")

The Bay trade didn't work nearly as well as the Nady deal did, but these were precisely the sorts of trades Huntington needed to make. The Pirates weren't going anywhere with the talent they had, and many of their highest-profile players were set to become free agents after 2009 or 2010 anyway. The Bucs weren't likely to get much in return for the core of a 67-win team, but it hardly hurt to try.

And so the trades continued. In August, they sent utilityman Jose Bautista to the Blue Jays for a Triple-A catcher, a trade that hurt, but only because Bautista's evolution into the game's most prolific home-run hitter was the most bizarre career transformation in baseball in at least a decade.

Bautista had hit sparingly in parts of five seasons in Pittsburgh. His development had likely been stunted by an injury-shortened 2003 season in the minor leagues and by Littlefield's Rule 5 Draft snafu, which forced Bautista to suit up for the Orioles, Devil Rays, Royals and Pirates in 2004 alone, playing infrequently along the way. By the time the Pirates traded Bautista, he was almost 28, and his chief assets were drawing walks and playing several positions, though he didn't play any of them very well. In other words, he didn't have much value, and so it was no surprise when every National League team passed on him as a waiver claim.

"We were looking for a super utility guy. A guy who could play second, third, outfield. And maybe a little pop," then-Blue Jays GM J.P. Ricciardi told MLB.com's Anthony Castrovince. "The trade was made under that premise. We thought if we played him more, he could hit 15-20 home runs."

In the midst of a mediocre 2009 season with the Jays, Bautista's hitting coach, Dwayne Murphy, encouraged him to change the timing of his leg kick, helping him on inside pitches. The Pirates had also noticed Bautista's timing issues, but they hadn't been able to explain the problem. "It never was explained to me in the way these guys did it. It didn't make sense in my head when they'd say you're getting ready too late," Bautista told SportsNet.ca. "They didn't pinpoint and explain it to me in a way that I would understand it the way [manager Cito Gaston] and Murph did."

Charlie Wilmoth

That Bautista failed to break through with the Pirates, then, was probably mostly a failure of coaching. Still, no one could have predicted he'd become baseball's best power hitters – although it *was* the sort of thing that seemed to happen to the Pirates.

The Bucs made another minor trade, sending Ronny Paulino to the Phillies for another mediocre catcher, Jason Jaramillo. Then, the following June, they shipped outfielder Nate McLouth to the Braves for pitchers Charlie Morton and Jeff Locke and outfielder Gorkys Hernandez.

It was the McLouth deal that really sent many non-Builder fans over the edge. Not only was McLouth popular, but management had signed him to a three-year extension only months before. I personally wasn't enamored of the trade (at Bucs Dugout, I called it "a bit of a grab bag"), but it made sense – McLouth wasn't old, but he probably wasn't young enough or talented enough to be an important part of the next good Pirates team. All three players the Bucs acquired had some promise, and the deal also opened center field for Andrew McCutchen, who made his big-league debut the next day. And McLouth, though he had won a Gold Glove Award in 2008, played below-average defense, which made him less of a star than he initially appeared.

Nonetheless, Pirates fans were incensed. "This is absolutely awful, and I might be done with the Pirates," wrote one Bucs Dugout commenter, in a response typical of many fans. "The FO continues to be a joke!" Fans and commentators delighted in pointing out that the 2008 outfield of Bay, Nady and McLouth had been the "most productive outfield in baseball," even though that trio's below-average defense was a big reason why the team's pitchers had struggled. Pirates fans passed around a YouTube video of a song called "It's over cuz you traded McLouth," featuring a young man hiccupping lines like "Ooh, the Pirates, freakin' jagoffs" and "Did you know that he won a freakin' Gold Glove?" over solo electric bass accompaniment. (Freakin' *rock*, dude.)

Huntington kept dealing. Later that month, he sent outfielder Nyjer Morgan and reliever Sean Burnett to the Nationals for outfielder Lastings Milledge and reliever Joel Hanrahan. In July, he traded Adam LaRoche to Boston for two minor-leaguers, then sent fan favorite Jack Wilson and frustrating starter Ian Snell to the Mariners for shortstop Ronny Cedeno, first baseman Jeff Clement and three minor-league arms. Then Freddy Sanchez went to the Giants for a pitching prospect, and pitchers Tom Gorzelanny and John Grabow headed to the Cubs for utilityman Josh Harrison and two pitchers.

Obviously, in Pittsburgh, this was attention-grabbing stuff. That the Pirates didn't get star-caliber talent back for their most experienced players bothered many fans. Hanrahan blossomed into a terrific closer for a couple years, and Morton, Locke, Tabata, Karstens, Morris and a few others turned out to be at least somewhat helpful. But many fans had unreasonable expectations about what the Pirates should have been able to get back for the core of a 67-win team. "Part of me regrets having said this, but it's not like we broke up the '27 Yankees," Huntington told ESPN's Jerry Crasnick. It was hard to fault the fans for their frustration, or for feeling like the trades were just business as usual, rather than an indicator of a major shift in strategy. It isn't easy to watch one's favorite team dismantle itself. But with the exception of Bay, none of the players the Pirates traded were worth much, and the Pirates' core hadn't been good enough to contend.

Huntington's performance in the trades was far from perfect. He cashed in many of the Pirates' trade chips on former top prospects like Andy LaRoche, Milledge and Clement. All had disappointed their previous teams, but all were young and interesting enough that at least one of them should have blossomed into something. None of them did.

But the trades were the right ideas. And Huntington was also doing important work in the draft and the farm system. The differences between Huntington's draft and development strategy and his predecessor's were enormous, and widely misunderstood – even in September 2012, Dejan Kovacevic absurdly claimed that Huntington's farm system wasn't much better than Littlefield's.

Charlie Wilmoth

The Pirates had been pouring ridiculous sums into amateur talent acquisition, and by 2012, they had an above-average farm system. From 2008 through 2011, they spent more than any other team on draft picks. That included over $6 million for No. 2 overall pick Pedro Alvarez in 2008, $6.5 million for No. 2 pick Jameson Taillon in 2010, $8 million for top overall pick Gerrit Cole in 2011, and $5 million for Josh Bell in 2011, a record for a second-round pick. They had built a new academy in the Dominican as well, and were paying more attention to international talent. By late 2012, their system included Cole and Taillon – two of the best pitching prospects in baseball – along with Bell, fellow outfielder Gregory Polanco, infielder Alen Hanson, and Mexican pitcher Luis Heredia, all of whom had star potential.

Again, though, it isn't as if there weren't legitimate criticisms to be made. It isn't enough to merely be willing to spend. (And that's primarily dictated by ownership anyway, rather than management – not that Pirates fans gave Bob Nutting much credit, either.) You've also got to pick the right players. Increasingly, Builders pointed to the farm system as evidence that wasn't happening, even though the farm system was strong overall. Despite historic draft expenditures, many of the Pirates' expensive big-bonus picks (particularly from the 2009 and 2010 drafts, in which they spent millions on flops like Zack Von Rosenberg, Trent Stevenson, Drew Maggi and Jared Lakind) weren't getting the job done. And many of the ones who *were* playing well were very early draft picks, like Cole and Taillon, or the recipients of enormous bonuses, like Bell and Heredia, who everyone knew were talented.

Huntington's decisions at the major-league level weren't particularly inspiring, either. He was developing an awful record with veteran acquisitions. Infielder Ramon Vazquez, signed prior to the 2009 season, became a bust almost immediately, and veteran relievers like Tyler Yates, Denny Bautista, Chris Bootcheck and Phil Dumatrait, all acquired in minor moves, weren't much better. Huntington did score early in his tenure when he signed first baseman and outfielder Garrett Jones to a minor-league deal – Jones never became a star, but he did become an important cog in the Pirates' offense. But as Wilbur Miller frequently points out, it's surprising that Huntington couldn't find a few more diamonds in the rough, especially after the Pirates' trades created lots of opportunities for lesser-known players.

Regardless, the 2009 Pirates went 62-99. That was only five fewer wins than the 67 or so the old core seemed to produce each year, and the 2009 Pirates wouldn't have played well even if all their old players had stuck around. But a 99-loss team is never fun to watch, and the Pirates, helmed by the borderline-comatose John Russell, looked downright listless.

2010 was even worse, as the Pirates finished 57-105. Before the season, the Pirates had acquired Akinori Iwamura from the Rays and installed him at second base; he played miserably and appeared heavier than he had been the previous season, and it later emerged that the Pirates didn't give him a physical exam before finalizing the trade. A few other moves – signing closer Octavio Dotel and lefty Javier Lopez to cheap big-league deals, and another reliever, D.J. Carrasco, to a minor-league contract – turned out better. But the struggles of any number of veterans acquired to help that year's team (Bobby Crosby, Ryan Church, Brendan Donnelly, Jack Taschner, Sean Gallagher, and others) were tough to take, and so were poor performances from a number of players the Pirates had acquired in trades, including Andy LaRoche, Jeff Clement, Charlie Morton and Daniel McCutchen.

In early May of that season, the Pirates were already 13-16 when they experienced one of the weirder plays of the streak. The Bucs were down 3-2 with the Cardinals in the eighth inning, and they had Andy LaRoche on third and Andrew McCutchen on first. Garrett Jones hit a ground ball back to Cardinals pitcher Trever Miller, and LaRoche got caught between third and home. As the Cardinals trapped LaRoche in a rundown, McCutchen scampered all the way to third. Catcher Yadier Molina chased LaRoche back to the bag, and then tagged McCutchen with both McCutchen and

LaRoche standing on third. The rules dictated that LaRoche had the right to the base, but he took a few steps toward the dugout anyway, thinking he was out. Molina applied the tag, completing the bizarre double play.

Odd, but these things happen, right? A Pirates fan sees a play like this not as a curiosity, or even as a temporary embarrassment, but as a thunderclap from a raincloud that follows her, Joe Btfsplk-like, everywhere she goes. The Pirates fan does can't easily shake off moments like these, because there's always another one waiting to pelt her. The first few years of Neal Huntington's tenure seemed to be full of them.

At the end of the season, the Pirates fired Russell after three years on the job, and replaced him with former Rockies manager Clint Hurdle. The Pirates didn't play perfectly after Russell left, but at least they seemed more vital.

Despite the Pirates' on-field struggles, Builders preached patience with Huntington. Many non-Builders were upset at the pace at which the plan unfolded, or they felt the Pirates should have kept players like Bay, Nady and McLouth. Builders pointed out that Dave Littlefield had left behind a disaster not only at the big-league level, but in the minors as well, and it would take many years for a new GM to put the team on firm footing. As the 2011 and 2012 seasons unfolded, though, even Builders became increasingly impatient as the Pirates fought through two disappointing years of pseudo-contention. (Later, we'll discuss the 2011 and 2012 seasons in detail.)

2012 was the Pirates' most successful season in more than a decade, but it increasingly seemed that the Pirates' deal-and-draft strategy might not have been as effective as Builders had hoped. The team still wasn't a legitimate contender, and the farm system, while strong overall, was littered with big-bonus busts from the Bucs' series of ultra-expensive drafts. "I felt like they were finally getting it right, and now it seems like they may not have," Ed Giles told me before the 2013 season. "There's this natural sense of disappointment."

Many Builders became increasingly skeptical of Huntington at around that time. "Initially, the thing that I liked was, like, 'Damn, he's doing all these things that I've been saying for years they need to do,'" says Wilbur Miller. "The strategies were everything I thought, for years, they should be doing."

Having a good strategy and being able to execute it, however, are two different things. "You have to make good baseball decisions," Miller says. "And I just felt like … Huntington didn't make good baseball decisions."

Miller argues that Huntington hadn't done a good job acquiring hitters. He also calls out Huntington's repeated signings of "washed-up bench players," like Brandon Inge, Matt Diaz, Ramon Vazquez, Chris Gomez and Ryan Church. "It's like, okay, he's a C-plus general manager, and the Pirates aren't going to survive with a C-plus general manager," Miller says.

I myself mostly gave up on Huntington during this period. I felt he hadn't gotten nearly enough out of the money the Pirates spent on the draft, and I questioned his offseason acquisitions, particularly the sad 2010-11 free-agent class of Diaz, Lyle Overbay, Kevin Correia and Scott Olsen.

Beginning with the acquisition of A.J. Burnett in early 2012, though, Huntington's decisions suddenly began to produce better results, culminating with a spectacular 2012-13 offseason, in which he signed Francisco Liriano to a bargain deal, acquired Russell Martin, and swapped Joel Hanrahan for Mark Melancon. At the same time, trade acquisitions Charlie Morton and Jeff Locke emerged as productive members of the Pirates' rotation, and Jason Grilli suddenly became a dominant closer. It's unclear how much of the spike in Huntington's success rate was due to variance and how much was due to improved performance on his part. But whatever the case, it looks like many Builders may have given up on Huntington a year too early.

In general, though, Builders are mostly perceived as being optimistic – other fans frequently call Builders "apologists," by which they mean apologists for the Pirates' front office and management. Most fans didn't show nearly the patience with Huntington or with the team that Builders did.

Antis

The opposite of Builders, which we'll call Antis, are – or maybe were? – everywhere. The reasons for the Pirates' losing streak were complex, and there was blame to be spread among different management teams and owners, as well as to the rules that govern Major League Baseball, which is the only American major pro sport without a salary cap. But the more simplistic Anti sees current Pirates owner Bob Nutting and his underlings Frank Coonelly and Neal Huntington as villains on about the same scale as Caligula or Jack the Ripper.

The Simplistic Anti's motivations are nebulous – maybe he (and the Simplistic Anti is nearly always a "he," for whatever reason) is just really impatient to see the Pirates win, but then again, maybe he just wants to see his viewpoint confirmed. The basic principles, though, rarely change. The team needs to spend more money, and that cheapskate Nutting won't open the checkbook. The team needs to put a winning product on the field *now*, or else Nutting should sell the team to Mark Cuban (the Dallas Mavericks owner and a Pittsburgh native) or some other quadrizillionaire.

To the Simplistic Anti, Nutting, Coonelly and Huntington are practically cartoon characters. Nutting is driven entirely by money, and Coonelly and Huntington are twin Smithers to Nutting's Mr. Burns. The Simplistic Anti's ideas about Nutting, in particular, can be feverish and bizarre. A prominent Anti once distributed a short story he had composed about Nutting attending a meeting in his hometown of Wheeling and being convinced to try coffee, which Nutting's character calls "the hot bean," for the first time. "What in tarnation would we want to do that for?" Nutting says (apparently because that's how people talk in Wheeling). Later, he suggests he'll select a new Pirates manager by drawing a name out of a coonskin cap.

Even some of Simplistic Antis' less obviously fantastical ideas can be well outside the realm of reality. In August 2010, for example, fans discussed the possibility that Nutting might have John Russell fired in the middle of the season, not because Nutting was tired of the Pirates' losing, but because he wanted to avoid the big bonus the Bucs would have to pay to the top overall pick in the draft if they didn't pick up the pace. The theory, a concoction of the *Post-Gazette*'s Bob Smizik (the Pied Piper of Antis), was an odd one. Spending heavily on the draft had been the core of the Pirates' strategy for three years running by that point. The Bucs happily dished out huge bonuses even in the late rounds, when they didn't have to.

Many fans didn't see it this way, but the performance of the Pirates' ownership improved dramatically almost immediately after Nutting replaced Kevin McClatchy as the public face of the team in 2007. After Dave Littlefield's embarrassing decisions to pass on Matt Wieters and trade for Matt Morris, Nutting canned him. The Pirates then completely changed direction in the draft, and they reestablished themselves as bidders for top talents in Latin America.

During their first few years with Nutting at the helm, the Pirates didn't spend much on major-league talent, but with the franchise in rebuilding mode, there wasn't much reason to. Why bloat the payroll for a 67-win team? Unless you're the Yankees, spending heavily on veterans is no way to build a franchise. Before the 2012 season, for example, the Angels signed Albert Pujols for $240 million and C.J. Wilson for $77.5 million. Before 2013, they signed Josh Hamilton for $125 million. They didn't make the playoffs in either season, and Mike Trout, a youngster developed through their farm system, was by far their most productive player in both years. The Pujols and Hamilton contracts already look like disasters. The 2012 Marlins and 2013 Blue Jays are also cautionary tales. The clearest path to sustained success – and, for the Pirates, probably the *only* path to sustained success – is building through the farm system. Forcing it simply doesn't work.

The Pirates' payroll will probably stay fairly low regardless of who's in charge. This isn't because Nutting is evil. It's because the Pirates don't have much money. PNC Park is small, attendance is generally low, and tickets are cheap. The Pirates don't serve a large population base. They don't control enough of their own parking. Without those things, huge payrolls aren't practical, or at least they aren't practical most seasons.

"I think there's a complete ignorance of what actually dictates how much money you can spend on a baseball team," Mueller says. "It's mainly predicated on the size of the market you're playing in and the TV deal you get."

There are a few Simplistic Antis who have been repeating slight variations on the same anti-Nutting theme on Twitter, blogs and message boards so persistently and for so long that it's amazing that they haven't burned out. Nothing seems to stop them, even when the only way for them to inject themselves into a conversation is with a non sequitur:

> Tweet: Colin Dunlap @colin_dunlap Seems very simple. If you get three times as many hits as the opposition and make no errors, you should win. Every single time.

> Response from Anti: @colin_dunlap Nutting Regime teams have a way of defeating all logic. It starts at the stingy top.

Mueller has called these kinds of fans "one-trick ponies," and notes that they've found homes on sports talk radio. "The hallmark of most radio callers is that they call in and they have their silly little agenda they want to establish, and that's it," he says.

Dry Land

The most seductive element of the Simplistic Anti's philosophy is that, in the most straightforward way possible, it was proven right over and over. The Pirates had 20 losing seasons in a row. Ipso facto, the Simplistic Anti could not be wrong. Of course, you had to ignore the issue of how much blame Nutting, Coonelly and Huntington deserved for the Pirates' problems, and how much went to Kevin McClatchy and Dave Littlefield, not to mention Major League Baseball's competitive-balance issues. And you might not be much fun at a dinner party. But with every losing season your favorite team had, you would feel better, not worse.

And so the Simplistic Anti's approach amounted to a heuristic. Confronted with 20 years of losing, some fans took the shortcut of assuming the Pirates' decisions were bad, rather than looking at the decisions themselves or worrying about their context. "People use [their approach to the team] as a type of validation," says Pat Lackey. "They are so used to the Pirates doing things wrong that they are unable to see them as doing something right until they have an actual quantitative result."

Antis were conditioned well. During the Littlefield era, the Pirates legitimately did almost nothing right. And if sports fandom is tied to our sense of identity, as we discussed in Chapter 3, then the Pirates spent 20 years *doing damage to our identities,* or at least some percentage of our identities. With our very notions of ourselves under attack, it likely wasn't easy to make measured decisions and fine distinctions. We were the socially defeated rat quivering in a box, and our situation was easier to manage if we could give the violent rat next to us a name.

Simplistic Antis can be scarcely more three-dimensional than they imagine Bob Nutting to be. The message board Change In Atmosphere (CIA), however, is one hangout for Antis whose views, or at least their views of the team, are often somewhat nuanced. (The website, like many angry corners of the internet, is filled with vicious misogyny and homophobia. I don't recommend visiting. But its members' views on the Pirates are worth examining, in an academic sort of way.) During the 2012 season, I created a screen name there to ask them what motivated them to stick with the team through 19 straight losing seasons.

Some of them didn't get to the point right away.

"Despite how much they bullshit, the Nuttings still run this team to profit first, and contend second," one user wrote. "And there's a litany of financial data – ranging from the exposed financial documents on Deadspin, to the Nuttings not following up with their promise to raise payroll with an increase in attendance, to the revelation that the Nuttings are the tenth-richest owners in MLB. Like it or not, the buck stops with them."

This is too simple a conclusion to draw from the body of evidence the user cites, so let's unpack that evidence a bit.

Some of the Pirates' financial documents were leaked to the media in August 2010. They showed that the Pirates were turning only a relatively modest profit even with extremely low payrolls. If anything, those documents suggested it would be very difficult for the Pirates to raise their payrolls to the levels many fans would like to see.

Bob Nutting (the only Nutting who's relevant here) did not explicitly promise to tie attendance to payroll, although, in February 2011, Frank Coonelly told Pirates Prospects something that sounded like that. And the Pirates *did* increase their payroll as attendance increased. Prior to the 2012 season, they signed McCutchen to a $51.5 million contract, agreed to take on $13 million of A.J. Burnett's salary in a trade with the Yankees, and signed Erik Bedard, Clint Barmes, Rod Barajas and Nate McLouth to contracts totaling about $20 million. (One can argue that these last four signings weren't the best ideas, certainly, but not that the Pirates were cheap for making them.) *During* the season, the Pirates acquired Wandy Rodriguez, taking on about $18 million in salary in the process. Then, in the winter, they signed Russell Martin to the largest free agent contract in team history – not a particularly big one, of course, but still bigger than any before.

Dry Land

Pirates Prospects calculates the 2012 total payroll was $59.5 million. The 2011 payroll was $53.4 million, for a difference of $6.1 million. The 2010 Pirates drew 1,613,399 million fans. In 2011, the Bucs drew 1,940,429. That's a difference of 327,030. The average ticket price at PNC Park in 2011 was $15.30, so an addition of 327,030 fans should have added about $5 million in additional revenue, plus concessions. $5 million is a drop in the bucket for a major-league team, and it's very much in line with the payroll increase that actually took place. That increase arguably was offset by a decrease in draft spending due to new rules that governed the 2012 draft, but the Pirates' $17 million in draft expenditures in 2011 easily broke MLB's record for a single year, strongly suggesting the Pirates knew the changes were coming and spent what they could while it was still possible. That shouldn't be held against them.

No one but the Pirates knows the exact numbers here, but an additional 327,030 fans in the one year after Coonelly's "promise" was made likely didn't result in a windfall for the Pirates, at least not in comparison with typical salaries for major-league veterans. And it's hard to square the idea that the Pirates broke a promise in 2012 by refusing to raise payroll with the facts that 1) they did raise payroll, albeit modestly; 2) they took on very substantial commitments in salary beyond 2012 by signing McCutchen and Barmes and trading for Burnett and Rodriguez; and 3) most of their key players in 2012 were relatively cheap. And the Pirates' payroll rose again in 2013, with the Associated Press reporting a total payroll of almost $75 million.

The Pirates' payroll *is* a legitimate issue. The payroll will likely continue to increase as players like Andrew McCutchen become more expensive, and as inflation drives payroll increases throughout the game. But we haven't yet seen it rise to the mid-market range, where many Pirates fans hope it will end up, at least in seasons in which the Bucs figure to be competitive. And what's happened in the 2013-14 offseason (with the Pirates allowing A.J. Burnett to leave for the Phillies shortly before this book went to press) gives little hope that it will in the near future, even with the

Pirates receiving more money from MLB's national TV deal. The Bucs' payroll continues to lag far behind fellow NL Central small-market teams in Cincinnati and Milwaukee, even though the Pirates finally have a competitive team in place.

The point, though, is that, even before the Pirates finally broke their losing streak in 2013, bashing Nutting, Coonelly and Huntington in the way most Antis did required them to sweep lots of complexity under the rug. It's not surprising that sports fans on a message board would overreach. But these sorts of arguments against Nutting and the front office are characteristic of many Pirates fans.

Despite their anger at the Pirates' ownership and management, Antis continue to follow the team, and follow it closely. The simplest reason why, of course, is that you don't just give up when things aren't going well. But another reason is that the Pirates' long tradition in Pittsburgh allows fans to feel that the team represents something greater than the person who currently owns it, or the people who run it.

"I liken my love for the Pirates to that of a child of a divorce," says one CIA user. "You may hate your former spouse (in this case, team management), but you still love your child (or in this case, the team)."

When Dave Littlefield ran the Bucs, one reason I kept rooting was that I believed that he did not represent the Pirates, but was instead an external agent wreaking havoc on a team that was somehow separate from him. Littlefield wasn't a Pirate, I thought. He was a cruel joke being played on them.

What is a team, really? The Pirates' ownership has changed since the streak started. The general manager has changed. *All* of the players are different. In fact, as I type this in January 2014, the only player *in all of professional baseball* who played on a winning Pirates team before the streak is 42-year-old Miguel Batista, who pitched in eight games for the Blue Jays' Triple-A affiliate in Buffalo in 2013. He notched two innings for the Pirates as a 21-year-old rookie in 1992.

Dry Land

Turnover of players and front office personnel mean the Pirates are not a person, or even a collection of people. "Loyalty to any one sports team is pretty hard to justify," as Jerry Seinfeld put it, pointing out that players frequently change teams. "You're actually rooting for the clothes."

Seinfeld was about 75 percent right. When you root, you're not primarily rooting for a group of people. But you're also not just rooting for the clothes. You're rooting for the team's history and its connection to its host city, and for times spent with loved ones at the stadium or around the TV. The Pirates have won five World Series in the city of Pittsburgh. Within the broad context of the Pirates' history, it's possible to see the 20-year losing streak as one very long aberration. The Pirates aren't losers. Look at what happened before.

The Antis' way of thinking makes sense as a response to the Pirates' decades of losing. But it doesn't permit much evolution of thought. Antis' conversations about the Pirates that aren't about Nutting tend to devolve into rants about the Bucs' front office, and their opposition to Neal Huntington tends to be the galvanizing topic. Most moves any front office makes are routine, and shouldn't be the basis for grand conclusions about the organization's future. But discussions about, for example, no-risk signings to fill minor-league rosters frequently turn into referenda on Huntington's perceived shortcomings.

Antis frequently brand commentators who praise the team, or who have positive or even ambivalent views of Huntington's job performance, as "apologists" (meaning that they apologize for the poor performance of the ownership or the front office) or worse.

Tim Williams of Pirates Prospects knows this firsthand, having been elevated to the status of a Huntington-level villain at Change In Atmosphere and in other corners of the web, mostly for defending Huntington.

I ask Williams why he thinks Pirates fans are so fixated on Huntington in particular. Fans, he says, "ignore that Major League

Baseball isn't like the NFL is," meaning that turning a weak MLB team around takes more time.

When one begins a job as a major-league general manager with a weak major-league roster and little talent in the minors, as Huntington did, it takes years to get the team into shape. That's especially true when it comes to the Pirates, who have far less money to work with than most teams, and, unlike the Steelers or Penguins, don't have the benefit of working within a league that has a salary cap. "If you can ignore … that Major League Baseball isn't really fair, then you get some simple arguments," Williams says.

Williams suggests that the "apologist" label with which he's frequently attacked is mostly a result of Antis' fixation on Huntington. "It suggests that they're somebody who [is] invested in selling people on the general manager, that they're not really interested in the team, they're just there to make excuses for the general manager," he says.

"But I noticed [that] the people who are saying 'apologist' are always the ones steering the conversation towards the general manager," Williams adds. "And the people who are being called apologists are always trying to talk about the players, and talk about the moves."

The Pirates' situation was such that many fans needed an enemy, and to put a face on their frustration. It was easier to simply blame the Pirates' front office rather than to acknowledge that, while Nutting, Coonelly and Huntington were all flawed, they were facing an extremely difficult task. They *do* deserve a portion of the blame for the length of the Pirates' streak, perhaps more than many Builders have typically assigned them. But they aren't the villains they're made out to be.

There are, of course, many fans who are sharply critical of the front office, and yet will acknowledge when Nutting and Huntington do things right. Bucs Dugout has a few regular commenters who fit that description. And on the other side, there are a few who exude nothing but rah-rah optimism about the team, as if the Pirates never had 20 straight losing seasons. And then, of course, there are dedicated fans whose interest in the team has little to do with what management does. But these fans don't dominate the conversation. It's the "apologists," who occasionally are overly optimistic about the team's management but mostly just want to address each move the Pirates make on its own terms, on one side. And on the other side, there are fans who are, or were, furious about the Bucs' losing streak and who needed a clear target for their anger.

Fatalists & Ironists

The Fatalist always expects the Pirates to be terrible. When things are going badly, that's to be expected. When things are going *well*, that's actually just a prelude to things going badly. In either case, the explanation for every win, every loss and every trade begins with the fact that *the Pirates are terrible.*

The Fatalist constantly braces for the worst, even when things are going well. "When the team is ... 11 games over .500, they just say, 'Ah, it's gonna come down,'" Mueller says. Given recent Pirates history, this isn't completely illogical. Fatalism is a kind of self-preservation, and the Fatalist was better equipped to deal with a long losing streak than someone who took every win or loss at face value.

There's a certain threshold beyond which hope replaces Fatalism, however. If the Pirates are five or 10 games above .500, that's one thing, and one might expect these kinds of self-preserving comments. But when the Bucs were 16 games above .500 in late July 2012, there were practically none. I looked through over 1,000 comments from Bucs Dugout on the night the Pirates went 16 games over, and I found only one comment that might qualify as Fatalist: "The Pirates keep winning but are not playing well," one commenter said. "This is different. But it would be reassuring if some players picked up their games."

Beyond that, the comments were overwhelmingly positive.

"I can't wait to make it [to PNC Park], for either win no. 82, or game 162. Whether these guys makes the playoffs or not it should be one helluva time," one wrote.

"Boys, that streak is in the dust," wrote another. "Need 24 wins; got 62 chances."

"Oh yeah," the commenter continued. "Nojinx nojinx."

Maybe Fatalism never dies after all.

Nearly all fans can relate to Fatalism to some degree. The supposed "curse" on the Red Sox until their 2004 World Series victory provides a case study. Boston cruised to a 3-0 series lead against the Cardinals. In Game 4, I couldn't quite believe they'd be able to seal the deal without fate intervening. With just one out to go, Sox reliever Keith Foulke fielded a comebacker, then jogged toward first and tossed the ball to Doug Mientkiewicz. I waited for Mientkiewicz to drop it, or perhaps to be struck by lightning. I'm sure many Red Sox fans, conditioned by Bill Buckner and decades of failure, felt the same way.

In 2012, the Pirates were 16 games above .500 on August 8. Rationally, it was absurd to believe that they wouldn't finish the season with a winning record. And yet, as a fan, it was impossible not to think they'd find a way to blow it. And sure enough, they did. Rooting for the Pirates can be like experiencing this feeling over and over, and not about lofty goals like winning the World Series, but about simpler ones like having a winning season or the Pirates not embarrassing themselves that day.

Irony also helped fans get through the streak. The Ironist roots from above the fray. "They have to justify the fact that they like something even though it's a bad product," Mueller says. "It's like justifying your affection for Nickelback." The Ironist watches bad baseball from above, making clear to herself, and perhaps to the world, that she is in some way distinct from the team and its faults.

I rooted for the team as an Ironist in the Littlefield era. Taking the Pirates at face value was impossible. I wanted the team to win, but I'm not sure the team truly wanted to, so I'd root in a complicated way. I'd root for my favorite players, of course – guys like Craig

Wilson, a slugger who was massively popular among sabermetrical-ly-oriented fans in the years before sabermetrics had much to say about fielding. But I'd also root *against* certain Pirates players – often veterans who were blocking Wilson, like Randall Simon and Jeromy Burnitz. If the Pirates were going to play terribly, I figured, they might as well do so in a way that confirmed my view of how baseball worked. Their general manager ought to receive some immediate feedback that his own way of looking at the game was bunk.

Contrarians

In Chapter 4, Eric Simons mentioned that contrarianism could be a part of what keeps Pirates fans rooting for the team. There's no doubt that contrarianism, or even defiance, can play a role – in a city obsessed with the Steelers and Penguins, passionately rooting for the Pirates can seem like an act of rebellion. But it's rare that contrarianism plays so great a part in a fan's interest in the team that his contrarianism defines him as a fan.

That's not to say that the Contrarian doesn't exist. A prominent one is Jed Pauls, a fan in his late thirties who's known on the internet as SoxDetox. Pauls grew up in New England as a Red Sox fan, and held Red Sox season tickets for nine years. The Red Sox came under new ownership in 2002 and embraced sabermetric analysis, leading to their World Series win in 2004. In the process, though, they renovated Fenway Park, which Pauls says made it more corporate.

"They labeled everything with trademarks," he says. "They have a new name for it – it's the 'America's Most Beloved Ballpark.' Big P.R. stuff. … It has a very self-important feel to it, as if it can't speak for itself." Pauls also points to the anonymous sources out of Boston who attacked Nomar Garciaparra and Terry Francona on their way out of town. For Pauls, rooting for the Red Sox became increasingly unpalatable.

Pauls and a friend began to discuss the possibility of switching allegiances. "We [followed] baseball so much, and we [didn't] even like the team that we like," he reflects. "It's just an unlikeable franchise that's disingenuous."

They decided to follow a small-market team, and Pauls chose the Pirates because he'd had one of the team's pillbox hats as a boy. Gold cap or no, though, the idea of switching allegiances from one team to another *and succeeding* would be difficult for most fans to fathom. I ask Pauls if his interest in the Pirates is purely intellectual, or if he feels an emotional connection to the team that goes beyond that.

He chuckles. "That's the daily dilemma for me," he says. "Do I really like this, or do I feel like I'm *supposed* to like this?"

Wait, what? Outside the Pittsburgh area, who the hell would feel like they're *supposed* to like the Pirates? It turns out, though, that there are many aspects of Pirates baseball that Pauls really does like. He's a fan of Clint Hurdle. He loves Pedro Alvarez's power. He likes the fact that the Pirates promote prospects to help the team, rather than using them primarily as trade chips. And he likes that he can concentrate on watching the game rather than whatever soap-opera nonsense happens to be swirling around Boston that season. He sees, overall, a kind of purity with the Pirates that he didn't get from the Red Sox.

That's real, not contrarian. And yet the roots of sports fandom are typically even simpler than valuing the purity of the game. We root because of where we grew up, or because of what we share with family and friends.

"All my friends are Red Sox fans, and they all think I'm a big jerk," Pauls says. "There is this piece of me that feels like I'm doing something unnatural, but ... humans have free will. I can do whatever the hell I want.

"I do feel like I'm abandoning a little bit of my history in my life. Some of the greatest memories of my childhood are going to Fenway Park for the first time, seeing Jim Rice play, watching the '86 World Series on the TV. I feel like I'm missing some of the connection to that. But then again, we're always distanced from our childhood."

Pauls might be a contrarian, but he sounds happier with his choices than do most fans who have rooted for the Pirates their whole lives.

What connects the various fan types is that, in the midst of 20 years of losing, it was very difficult to root straightforwardly. Builders, Antis, Fatalists, Ironists and Contrarians didn't agree on much, but for most of them, fandom needed to be more complex than turning on the TV and hoping for the best. It was difficult to root for the Pirates without a reason to continue, like the promise of a better future, or hatred of the team's ownership and front office, or one's own sense of whimsy. The various survival strategies Pirates fans employed sometimes put them at odds with one another. But it's hard to blame them. The Pirates and Major League Baseball had marooned them, and it's not surprising that they sometimes struggled to maintain order while they waited to be rescued.

Chapter 7

On July 8, 2011, the Pirates were one game behind the Milwaukee Brewers and the St. Louis Cardinals for the NL Central lead. A crowd of 37,140 crammed into PNC Park on a pleasant night to see the Bucs take on the Chicago Cubs. With two outs in the eighth inning, the Pirates were down 4-3 with two men on, and Josh Harrison tied the game with a single up the middle.

Then came rookie catcher Michael McKenry, the very personification of the baseball underdog. McKenry had recently joined the Pirates from the Red Sox' Class AAA team after the Bucs' top three backstops all went down with injuries, and he was still looking for his first homer after 69 career at-bats. He was generously listed at 5-foot-10, and when he'd played in the Rockies organization, fans had nicknamed him "Quadzilla." His body type, ready smile and receding hairline made him look more like an overeager bank teller than a professional athlete.

Cubs closer Carlos Marmol threw a fastball for a called strike one. McKenry fouled off another heater for strike two. Marmol then went after McKenry with one slider after another. McKenry fouled off four straight, then fouled off another fastball. And then Marmol threw a slider that broke right down the middle. McKenry hit it a mile, and it landed deep in the seats in left field.

The home crowd exploded. Andrew McCutchen hugged McKenry upon his return to the dugout, and his teammates coaxed him to climb the dugout steps for a curtain call. Joel Hanrahan recorded a 1-2-3 ninth to finish off the Cubs, and the Pirates improved to 46-42 on the season.

If you could go back in time to, say, October 2003, and ask Pirates fans what the most memorable moment from that season had been, they probably would have said Randall Simon and Sausagegate. In 2007, it might have been the firing of Dave Littlefield or Jim Tracy. In 2008, it might have been the trade of Xavier Nady or Jason Bay.

In 2011, though … well, actually, it would almost certainly be Jerry Meals' blown call in the 19th inning on July 26 in Atlanta, after which the Pirates never recovered. But there were big, positive, dramatic moments in there too. And not just isolated, any-given-weeknight moments, but moments that really mattered, or felt like they did. Pirates fans hadn't experienced moments like these in more than a decade.

The 2011 season didn't *seem* like it would feature that sort of excitement. The Bucs had won just 57 games the year before, thanks in part to a team defense that had done a miserable job supporting a mediocre pitch-to-contact starting rotation. Then, in the 2010-11 offseason, the Pirates had spent $15 million to sign Lyle Overbay, Matt Diaz, Kevin Correia and Scott Olsen.

Overbay, Diaz and Correia were all marginal veterans who were unlikely to help much, while Olsen was a marginal younger pitcher with anger issues. Overbay would become the Pirates' starting first baseman, a role that didn't suit him, given his age (he would turn 34 in January 2011) and his declining offense. Diaz looked like he might help the Pirates somewhat against left-handed pitching, but that was all. Correia was coming off a horrific season in pitcher-friendly San Diego, and he had little hope of doing more than eating innings in the back of the Bucs' rotation. And Olsen, who had struggled through shoulder trouble the previous season, didn't look like he'd be a significant factor, at least not on the field. He had a long history of causing trouble off it, with a résumé that included fighting with a Marlins teammate, flipping off a fan in

Milwaukee, and requiring the use of a Taser when he kicked police officers who were trying to arrest him for a DUI. (Olsen never ended up playing for the Pirates, but he did show flashes of Derek "Operation Shutdown" Bell when he pointedly told the *Post-Gazette*'s Colin Dunlap that if the Bucs wanted him to pitch out of the bullpen, they would have to "have a conversation" with him.)

These were, in short, depressing signings that had more in common with the Joe Randa- and Randall Simon-type acquisitions Dave Littlefield preferred than with anything a contending team would normally be doing. Unlike many of Littlefield's annual signings of over-the-hill vets, Huntington's 2011 crop wasn't blocking any good young talent, a crucial distinction. But there was also no reason to expect Overbay, Diaz, Correia or Olsen to even be average. Fan reaction to the signings ranged from indifference to annoyance. "If the Royals did this exact signing, we'd all be laughing at them," wrote one fan in response to the Overbay deal. Expectations heading into the season were low.

The Pirates beat the Cubs on Opening Day, then took two of their next three. But a week later, a tiny crowd (officially listed at 8,755, the smallest in the history of PNC Park) saw Shaun Marcum and the Brewers four-hit the Bucs in a 6-0 shutout. By the next day, the Pirates were in a hole with a 5-7 record, and it didn't look like they'd climb too far out of it. After a week, they got two-hit by Florida's Josh Johnson and two relievers; the following day, Ricky Nolasco and Edward Mujica shut them out again. The Marlins completed the sweep by pelting James McDonald. At the end of April, the Pirates were 12-15.

The Bucs rumbled back, taking series against Colorado, San Diego and Houston to return to .500. After they beat the Dodgers 4-1 to break the .500 barrier at 18-17, though, they lost six in a row.

The names were different, but the character of the team seemed typical – a few promising youngsters, like Andrew McCutchen, Neil Walker, Pedro Alvarez and McDonald; a nice reliever or two; and then a bunch of players like Correia, Jeff Karstens and Daniel McCutchen who were competent placeholders at best, filler at worst. *Then*, of course, there were players who couldn't even be damned with praise that faint. And so, in mid-May, when the Pirates got swept in Milwaukee, you could forgive fans who had already left them for dead.

"You could definitely see, 'Same old Pirates, season's over, they won't get back to .500,' and having followed the team so many years myself, that kind of attitude made sense to me," says David Todd, who hosted the Pirates' post-game radio show that year.

But the Pirates' season wasn't over. They won four in a row, and after dropping one game to the Tigers and two to the Braves, they took two of three from the Cubs at Wrigley Field, punctuating their series win with a 10-0, four-homer rout. They then headed to New York, where they split a four-game set against the Mets.

The Bucs returned from their week-long road trip at 26-29, and it was back at PNC that their 2011 season really started to gather steam. It was early June, right when the school year ends, and the sun begins to dry the spring rains. Games at PNC Park began to feel different. The Bucs took two out of three against a powerhouse Phillies team before three uncharacteristically enormous crowds, including 39,441 for a Saturday-night game in which Charlie Morton and Andrew McCutchen led the Bucs to a 6-3 victory. Many of those were Phillies fans, which is typical during Phillies series, but the excitement in the air was as palpable as the lines for concessions were impossible – PNC Park just wasn't used to hosting so many people. Walking about the main concourse at the ballpark was like trying to get through the Fort Pitt Tunnel at rush hour.

It was a good problem to have, at least if you were the Pirates. Personally, one aspect of PNC Park I'd always liked was how quiet it was. I felt like the local alt-weekly had just given my neighborhood bar a glowing review, and now the place was filled with trendy folks from across town.

After the series victory against Philadelphia, the Pirates took two in a row from the Diamondbacks to get to 30-30. A 30-30 record might not sound like much, but Bucs fans in 2005 had viewed 30-30 as a milestone.

The 2011 Pirates didn't stop at 30-30, however. They lost three of their next five, but then came a three-game set against a miserable Astros team. Jeff Karstens defeated Bud Norris in a pitchers' duel in the first game, and then Charlie Morton and James McDonald earned victories as the Pirates completed the sweep.

The Bucs then got swept themselves, by the Indians; the last game of the series was a frustrating 5-2, 11-inning loss in which journeyman reliever Tim Wood allowed a walk-off, three-run homer to Cord Phelps. It looked then like interleague play, which had been a bugaboo for the Pirates in the past, would be one again in 2011. Interleague games turned up on the schedule in June, just as the Pirates usually faded from relevance. And American League competition tended to be tough.

After dropping a game against Baltimore, though, the Pirates won four in a row, then didn't lose a series for another month. After taking two of three from the Orioles, the Pirates did the same against the Red Sox and Blue Jays, with the Orioles and Red Sox series victories coming at PNC Park, in front of increasingly enthusiastic crowds. They split a four-game set on the road against the Nationals, then headed home and took two of three from the Astros.

Then came McKenry's home run. A week later, in their first game after the All-Star break, the Bucs beat the Astros to claim a share of first place. They then won three of their next four games to improve to 51-44.

The mood among Pirates' fans at this point was different than at any point in the last decade. Most years, you'd drift through the summer looking for reasons to watch. This could be annoying and existentially draining, but if you were in the right mood, it could also be strangely calming, knowing you were watching something that fundamentally didn't matter (assuming sports really matter in the first place). Going to a game was a little like going to, say, a car show, or the county fair, or idly watching a kickball game in progress while walking through a park. You could enjoy little details of a game, and the atmosphere of the game itself, without fretting about its cosmic significance. This probably wasn't a great way to sustain your fandom over the long term, but if you caught yourself at just the right moment, it could feel rather nice.

In 2011, or at least for a couple months of it, that attitude bit the dust. One night, a friend who I could not recall ever having interest in baseball asked me if I wanted to meet him at a bar to watch "the game."

"The game"? What was he talking about? Had the Steelers' preseason started already?

It hadn't. It was simply the dawning of a new era in which the Pirates seemed relevant again. The stands at PNC Park, so often nearly empty, were frequently packed. And the Pirates' season, so often an afterthought by June, stayed in the public consciousness deep into the summer.

"People were really excited about it," Todd says, noting that even the once-ubiquitous criticism of the team faded away. "I had a couple consistent callers who still would badmouth the Pirates, but you even saw the tone of *that* change. Those people, rather than changing their view, just didn't call anymore."

"I'm a believer," one fan on my website wrote in early July. "[T]hey have a chance to make the playoffs. This year. That feels weird to even be typing, but I like it."

"Watching McKenry do that is just another reason that something magical is happening out there," said another, following McKenry's homer off Marmol.

Local TV ratings rose, and stores sold far more Pirates memorabilia than they expected to. "We go into a season not really prepared for success," Hometowne Sports' Linda Meyer told the *Tribune-Review*'s Joe Starkey. "But there's a huge demand right now. I think the city would be all over the Pirates being very successful."

For a short time, the Pirates were able to maintain the magic. They won another series against hapless Houston, and the first of those wins catapulted them into first place in the NL Central. They then took two of three against the Reds, with Morton and McDonald each leading the Pirates to shutouts.

Heading into their July 26 19-inning debacle against the Braves, the Pirates were 53-47 and still tied for first in their division. Thanks to a rain delay, the Bucs and Braves' game the previous night had gone well past midnight, and it was about to happen again.

The game began straightforwardly enough, with Jeff Karstens allowing three runs in five innings and Tommy Hanson giving up three through six. After that, though, there were so many remarkable story lines that it's difficult to even list them all – the ejections of Atlanta's Fredi Gonzalez and Nate McLouth; the Pirates' Jason Grilli stranding seven runners in three innings of relief; Atlanta infielder Martin Prado's 0-for-9; Braves pitcher Cristhian Martinez's brilliant six-inning, 88-pitch relief outing, which took the Braves through the 16th inning; and so on.

By the time Scott Proctor finally relieved Martinez in the 17th, Pirates reliever Daniel McCutchen was himself piling up one scoreless inning after another. McCutchen had gutted his way through five frames by the time he came to the mound again in the 19th.

With one out in the bottom of the inning, McCutchen walked Julio Lugo, then gave up a line-drive single to Jordan Schafer. Schafer moved to second on defensive indifference, taking away the double play.

Then Proctor, the last pitcher left in the Braves' bullpen, came to the plate and quickly got into an 0-and-2 hole. He grounded a McCutchen slider towards third, and Pedro Alvarez threw home, beating Lugo by a mile.

McKenry stood a few feet in front of the plate and outside the base path, but he received the throw, swung his arm around and tagged Lugo on the knee. He showed home plate umpire Jerry Meals the ball, then looked toward Schafer at third.

Meals, however, had decided that McKenry had somehow missed the tag, and called Lugo safe, ending the game. Lugo was visibly shocked at Meals' decision, instinctively tapping home plate again immediately after Meals made the call, as if it had completely changed his impression of what had happened.

Dry Land

At that point, my eyes and mind were shot, having watched the game from the beginning, and it became clear that, for all the remarkable things that had happened, the most amazing aspect of the game was how unbelievably *long* it had been. As it turned out, it was the longest game the Pirates had ever played, at six hours and 39 minutes.

In the moment, it seemed distinctly possible that Meals had ended the game when he did because he was exhausted – a beer-league softball move. *My knees are killing me. Let's go home.* That surely wasn't the case, of course, but that was the first thing my addled brain could come up with to explain a decision that looked so thoroughly, unmistakably wrong.

"I saw the tag, but he looked like he oléd him and I called him safe for that," Meals told the media after the game.

"I think that maybe it was a tougher call than some Pirates fans give Jerry Meals credit for," Pat Lackey says, and he's right. McKenry *did* visibly touch Lugo's knee, but replays made clear that Meals' in-the-moment interpretation wasn't completely without basis. McKenry's glove came dangerously close to missing the runner.

Still, it was a blown call. Even Meals later admitted there was a chance he had gotten the call wrong. "I looked at the replays and it appeared he might have got him on the shin area," he said. "I'm guessing he might have got him, but when I was out there when it happened, I didn't see a tag."

If you were one of the few who sat through the entire six-and-a-half hours, it was easy to imagine the Pirates' house-of-cards season coming crashing down as a result. The Pirates' streak of losing seasons had begun with a play at the plate in Atlanta (Sid Bream's slide, which eliminated the Bucs from the 1992 NLCS), and I wrote that night that it seemed possible that their 19th straight losing season would be triggered by another one.

That's exactly what happened. Or at least that's how it looked. In reality, the 2011 Pirates weren't very good, and their run at contention was fueled by luck and by a number of overachieving pitchers. The Bucs probably would have collapsed anyway. But the

Meals call was a gigantic moment, and after it, the Pirates weren't the same.

Fans had mixed reactions to what happened next. "The saving grace was that the Steelers were in camp, and the Steelers' season starts in September, so it wasn't necessarily the vitriol that you had seen in years past," Todd says. "It was, 'Well, same old Pirates, but they kept me entertained for the summer, and now I have the Steelers.'"

Many fans who stuck around took the Pirates' fall hard, though. "It almost felt like everything was collapsing back to square one at that point," Lackey says.

That was my feeling, too. Due to a scheduling quirk, I had covered the Meals game for three different websites. I didn't finish until 3:30 in the morning, at which point I was ravenous and bleary-eyed, and feeling like a fool for caring about any of it – the game, the Pirates' season, baseball in general, whatever. The first one was prematurely over, and I was pretty sure the second one was too.

As the Pirates' season did, in fact, fall apart over two long months, I felt exhausted. I was making a living as a writer at the time, and I'd spent the summer writing about 3,000 words about sports each day. Perhaps a majority of those words had been about the Pirates. I felt like I had been tricked. It had been hard to believe, intellectually, that the Pirates were a playoff team, but it hadn't been hard, emotionally, to get wrapped up in that possibility.

What made it worse was that when the Pirates fell, they fell *hard*. Not only did they not look like a playoff team, but there were plenty of nights when they didn't look like they could beat the Williamsport Crosscutters. After winning the last game of their series against Atlanta, the Bucs began a ten-game losing streak, losing every game in consecutive series against the Phillies, Cubs and Padres.

The first two games against San Diego represented the season's nadir. In the first, the Pirates lost 15-5 as Jeff Karstens allowed nine runs and the struggling Pedro Alvarez put up one of the worst single games by a Pirate that season, going 0-for-5 while grounding into three double plays. The second was a 13-2 blowout at the hands of opposing pitcher Cory Luebke who, along with two relievers, struck out 11 Pirates and walked none. Frustrating Bucs shortstop Ronny Cedeno double-clutched a throw to allow a key hit, and made two errors.

"It can't get any worse," reliever Chris Resop told the media after emerging from a players-only meeting. "If there's a positive, it can't get any worse."

In the midst of the losing streak was the July 31 trading deadline, and the Bucs were still contending when it happened, so they approached it as buyers for the first time since … well, the ludicrous Matt Morris deal. But they were buying *and* contending for the first time since August 1997, when they traded for veteran infielder Shawon Dunston.

In need of a first baseman, the Pirates sent a prospect to Baltimore for former Cubs star Derrek Lee. The next day, they acquired outfielder Ryan Ludwick from the Padres for cash or a player to be named. They released Lyle Overbay days later, then traded Matt Diaz to the Diamondbacks in a minor deal at the end of August. The Pirates thus upgraded two positions by correcting mistakes they'd made the previous offseason. Soon after the Bucs acquired Lee, however, he missed nearly a month with a fractured wrist, and he watched most of the Pirates' collapse from the bench, though he hit brilliantly when he returned. Ludwick was a non-factor – he didn't find his stroke again until he signed with the Reds the next season.

In any case, the Pirates were falling apart before Lee and Ludwick arrived. Most fans moved on as it became clear that the air was out of the balloon, and PNC Park crowds dwindled as summer ended. My own writing descended into absurdity, as I found it increasingly difficult to take the games at face value. I wrote the recap of the 13-2 Padres game from the perspective of a 12-year-old in attendance to watch the rock band Train, who played at PNC after the game. But that sort of silliness only helped so much. It can be rewarding to wring humor out of a bad situation. But it's hard to do, day after day, and the ends of Pirates seasons can feel like endurance exercises. 2011 was particularly tough, since the ten-game losing streak whipped the rug out from under the Bucs' season so quickly.

The Pirates ended the losing streak with a win in San Francisco, and they took two of three there. But next came a series at Miller Park in Milwaukee, and though the interleague bugaboo disappeared in 2011, the Bucs' Miller Park bugaboo didn't. The Brewers swept the Bucs to leave them at seven games below .500.

The Bucs then treaded water throughout a ten-game homestand before returning to the road, where their season got even worse. They lost three of four in St. Louis, then got swept in Houston, where they were soundly beaten by a collection of players no one had ever heard of. (Henry Sosa. J.D. Martinez. Jimmy Paredes. Bryant Young. Matt Downs. Angel Sanchez. I made up one of those names – does it even matter which one?) The Pirates then won a three-game set against the Cubs and got revenge by winning two of three against the Astros, but then a sweep by the Marlins left them 14 games below .500.

The Bucs had briefly flirted with contention, but she was so far gone now, she'd started a family with another man. As if to make that clear, the Pirates then dropped series against the Cardinals, Dodgers and Diamondbacks, flailing before finally ending their season by losing two out of three at Miller Park.

The Bucs' final record of 72-90 was pretty close to what they deserved. Their Pythagorean record (a measure of the won-loss record suggested by their runs scored and allowed) was 70-92. They finished 14th in the National League in runs scored, and 11th in runs allowed, and those figures made sense when one took a hard look at their roster. They had gotten very little out of their corner infielders, and they'd had to use eight catchers, turning to minor-league veterans like Dusty Brown and Wyatt Toregas after Chris Snyder, Ryan Doumit and Jason Jaramillo all got hurt. Their starting rotation was, essentially, four No. 3 starters (Paul Maholm, James McDonald, Jeff Karstens and Charlie Morton) and a No. 5 (Kevin Correia). Other than closer Joel Hanrahan, none of their relievers were anything to write home about.

Dry Land

They were, in other words, a bad team, and if their wins had been distributed a bit differently, they never would have teased us in the first place. As it stood, Pirates fans got their first taste of late-summer contention since 1997. That summer's dog days were awful. But as hard as the Pirates' collapse was to take, it wouldn't be long before the Bucs would contend more legitimately.

Chapter 8

After the 2011 collapse, the 2011-2012 offseason began inauspiciously, as the Pirates bid adieu to Paul Maholm, Ryan Doumit, Chris Snyder, Ronny Cedeno, Derrek Lee and Ryan Ludwick. It looked like the Pirates were "set to downgrade [a] 90-loss team," as one internet article put it. Turnover of veteran players each offseason is inevitable, but the departures of Maholm and Cedeno, in particular, seemed troubling, since the Pirates had reasonable team options on those players in 2012 and had a history of wasting money on free agents.

The Pirates could have kept Maholm, a reliable mid-rotation starter, for $9 million ($9.75 million minus a $750,000 buyout) in 2012. That they decided not to was perhaps defensible as a pure dollars-and-cents move, but there wasn't much reason to think they could do better if they spent the money elsewhere, given their previous misadventures in the free-agent market. The Bucs had done fairly well acquiring veterans to fill bullpen spots – Dotel, Javier Lopez, D.J. Carrasco, Jose Veras, Jason Grilli, and so on. But they had struggled to find good position players and starting pitchers.

Some fans suggested that Neal Huntington had an uncanny ability to stock his bullpen and yet lacked that ability with other types of players, but that wasn't quite right. Relievers are, on average, less important than position players or starting pitchers, and relievers also tend to experience more year-to-year variation in performance. That makes most of them fungible, so it's not uncommon for decent veteran relievers to bounce from team to team on cheap one-year contracts.

The Pirates could afford to sign decent relievers to short, cheap deals. Rarely could they afford to sign good position players or starting pitchers, who usually required more money and longer commitments. Also, players who had choices about whether to sign with the Pirates or to take a similar offer from another team might well pick the other team. (If *you* could sign with a team with 19 straight losing seasons or *any other team*, who would you pick?) Add in the fact that free agents (who usually have six-plus years of big-league service time) tend to be past their primes, and the free agent market amounted to a disaster for the Pirates – for all player types *except* relievers.

So when the Bucs passed on the chance to keep Cedeno at $2.8 million ($3 million minus a $200,000 buyout) and especially Maholm at $9 million, some Pirates fans fretted. Cedeno and Maholm weren't great players, but they were younger than typical free agents. And if the team exercised Cedeno and Maholm's options, they'd have no choice but to come play for the Bucs. Instead, a team that had faded badly down the stretch in 2011 was about to jettison talent right before entering an offseason free-agent market that had crushed it in the past.

The results of the Pirates' gamble were mixed. Cedeno and Maholm signed with other teams for significantly less than the costs of their options, suggesting that, on paper, the Pirates had made the right moves in letting them go. (Although Maholm, at least, told MLB Network Radio he never even received an offer from the Pirates before signing a one-year, $4.75 million deal with the Cubs.)

But how would the Pirates replace them? They began by signing starting pitcher Erik Bedard to a $4.5 million deal that looked like a good idea at the time. Bedard, who would turn 33 in March, was older than Maholm, but he had a track record of performing well when he could stay healthy, which admittedly was rarely. Bedard was a poor bet to eat innings, but he provided the Pirates with a bit of upside they wouldn't have had with Maholm.

To replace Cedeno, the Bucs signed Clint Barmes to a two-year, $10.5 million contract. That Barmes' deal was, at the time, the largest free agent contract in the Pirates' history says far more about the Bucs than about the signing itself, but the deal was still a questionable one for an aging infielder whose main offensive asset was right-handed power that wouldn't play well in PNC Park. The idea was that Barmes' excellent defense would help the Pirates' pitching staff, while providing a steadier hand that the erratic Cedeno.

The Pirates kept moving, replacing Doumit and Snyder with 36-year-old Rod Barajas, who signed for one year and $4 million. Barajas, who rarely got on base, was no prize, but in a catching market that had little else to offer, and with Michael McKenry as the only viable catching option left in the organization, the Pirates needed to get *someone*.

The Bucs also signed Nate McLouth for no obvious reason. McLouth had, of course, been a fan favorite in his previous tenure with the Pirates, but his 2010 and 2011 seasons with the Braves suggested that his skills had diminished. The Pirates threw $1.75 million at him anyway. The Bucs also acquired righty first baseman Casey McGehee in a deal with Milwaukee.

The Pirates' offseason, mostly uninspiring to that point, took a big turn for the better in February, when they traded two fringe prospects to the Yankees for starting pitcher A.J. Burnett, with New York paying $20 million of the $33 million on the last two years of his contract. The Yankees were eager to get rid of Burnett, who had posted ERAs of 5.26 and 5.15 in his previous two seasons. Even at age 35, though, Burnett had a good fastball and a strong strikeout rate, and he appeared more likely to succeed with the Pirates, as he moved from the relatively homer-happy Yankee Stadium to homer-suppressing PNC Park, and from the AL East to the weaker NL Central.

The Burnett move was shrewd, and it turned what had been a mediocre offseason into a modestly promising one. But newly acquired veterans can only help a team like the Pirates so much. And so the Pirates went into spring training improved, but only modestly so. A 72-90 team now looked like it might win 75 games. The rotation had improved (Burnett was a clear upgrade, and Bedard looked like one too), but the signings of Barmes and McLouth weren't particularly promising.

Early in spring training, the Pirates signed Andrew McCutchen to a six-year, $51.5 million extension, with an option for 2018. It was a terrific, and tremendously important, deal aimed at the organization's future. But it didn't appear to have much direct impact on the 2012 team, since the Pirates had controlled McCutchen's rights through 2015 anyway. So the Bucs' offseason boiled down to the additions of Bedard, Barmes, Barajas and Burnett (you could imagine the Killer B's T-shirts being printed, although, as it turned out, Burnett was the only one with much "killer" left in him) along with McLouth. Thanks to Burnett, that was a better offseason than I had expected, but it hardly appeared to be a transformative one.

For a short time, it looked like the Pirates might struggle to match even their modest 2011 win total. Roy Halladay and Jonathan Papelbon two-hit them in the season opener, and, after the Bucs took the next two games to win the opening series against the Phillies, they lost five in a row to the Dodgers and Giants. The first of those losses was a five-hit effort by Clayton Kershaw and two relievers. The next day, a Wednesday, the Bucs only got six hits. On Thursday, they had eight, but managed only two runs against Chris Capuano, who struck out seven batters and walked none. On Friday they only got one hit against Matt Cain, and that was by pitcher James McDonald.

Toss in an error-filled 4-3 loss on Saturday, and Pirates fans weren't exactly bubbling over with optimism for the long season. "You wonder, is it the dead-ball era again?" David Todd says. "When I was [predicting] 69 wins, and you see the team come out of the chute like that, you wonder if you missed it high by ten."

The Bucs had pitched very well (Bedard, Jeff Karstens and Kevin Correia had all come up big in those first eight games), but their offense was miserable. Barajas was 1-for-20 after those eight games; Barmes was 3-for-26. Jose Tabata was 4-for-30. Neil Walker was 5-for-29. Pedro Alvarez, after a miserable 2011 season and then a spring training so bad that a scout told *Baseball America* that "[i]f you didn't know he was Pedro Alvarez, you'd [No Prospect] him," was 1-for-19 with 12 strikeouts.

That basic pattern persisted throughout April, as the Pirates faced one tough pitcher after another, and did little against them. By the end of the month, Barajas had an OPS of .406, and Barmes was at .469; the Pirates only had a .618 OPS as a team.

Thanks to brilliant performances from the pitching staff, though, the Bucs kept their heads above water. Burnett and McDonald began to look like top rotation options, and Jason Grilli led an excellent bullpen with a ridiculous 15 strikeouts and one walk in eight innings pitched. The Bucs finished the month 10-12, but given the strength of the pitching they faced (taking on Roy Halladay, Cliff Lee, Clayton Kershaw and Matt Cain in one seven-game stretch was no picnic) and the offense's awful performance (which somehow made those pitchers look even better than they were), it could have been much worse.

It wasn't uncommon for the Pirates to perform rather well, or at least passably, early in the season. On May 1, 2011, they were 13-15. In 2009, they were 11-11. In 2007, they were 12-13. These weren't *good* performances, and in some of the years in between, their Aprils were terrible. But the broad trend was that the Pirates would play reasonably well for a couple months, and then fade from view in June or, if we were very lucky, a bit later.

Still, even in the first six weeks of the 2012 season, fans squabbled about the Pirates' supposed lack of commitment to winning and demanded they make a big trade for a veteran, as if it had been clear at that point that the team was a contender. That the Pirates' pitching was a pronounced strength and their hitting a pronounced weakness early in the season convinced many fans that the Pirates needed to trade for a hitter, post-haste. Never mind that it was May, and most teams aren't ready to trade top talents that early. Also, the Pirates had few good prospects in the upper levels of the minors at the time. So it would have been difficult, at that point, to trade for a difference-making hitter without dealing a top prospect, or sending off some of the big-league pitching that had kept the team afloat to that point. Neal Huntington suggested to the *Post-Gazette* that it was difficult to trade in May and that he expected the hitting to improve on its own. His comments infuriated an antsy fan base, but his prediction turned out to be correct.

That didn't happen right away, however. The Pirates drifted a bit in early May, losing series to the Cardinals and Reds and dropping to 12-16. In the last game of those series, Mat Latos and Cincinnati three-hit the Bucs. A week later, Justin Verlander took a no-hitter into the ninth inning in the Bucs' first game of a series in Detroit, with the Pirates' only hit coming when Josh Harrison reached for an 87-MPH slider and hit a soft line drive. The Bucs had yet again avoided being no-hit, but there already been several occasions where they had come perilously close.

The Bucs wound up dropping two of three against the Tigers and two of three against the Mets, but a home series against the awful Chicago Cubs turned out to be just what the doctor ordered. Burnett and four relievers shut down the Cubs offense in a 1-0 win in the series opener. The second game was tied 2-2 in the ninth when Chicago reliever Rafael Dolis allowed a single and two walks to load the bases, then plunked Matt Hague in the side with a 96-MPH fastball. Pirates fans could surely have related to the pain Cubs fans must have felt – it was the Cubs' 11th straight loss, and not only were they losing, they were doing it creatively, much as the Pirates had in past years. Now, Pirates fans got to watch their team's *opponents* do that kind of thing.

And Bucs fans got more out of the Cubs series than schadenfreude. Before the series, the Bucs were 20-24, on their way to another bland, 70-win type of season. After a three-game sweep and a win against the Reds, the Pirates were 24-24, just three games back of the division lead. There were other triumphs as well: in the last game of their series against the Cubs, Andrew McCutchen, Pedro Alvarez and Garrett Jones all homered in an offensive outburst of a kind that had been tough to come by earlier in the season.

The Bucs sailed into June with the wind at their backs. They arrived at Miller Park, where they'd gone 1-8 in 2011 and 2-7 in 2010, and won a series thanks to a rejuvenated offense, piling up four home runs in the series finale. They then headed to Cincinnati and took two of three, with one of the victories coming when Clint Barmes and Michael McKenry hit back-to-back doubles off Reds closer Aroldis Chapman, who hadn't allowed an earned run all season.

Then it was off to interleague play, where previous seasons had gone to die. This one didn't, as the Bucs swept the Royals. The Pirates lost four straight after that, but the two games that followed were revelatory. In the first, Alvarez, who had a meager .627 OPS to that point, hit a solo shot to right in the second inning, then blasted off to center in the ninth. The next day, he hit a three-run homer in the fourth, then came up with two men on yet again the next inning. The Indians turned to Esmil Rogers, a hard-throwing but erratic righty who the Rockies had recently designated for assignment. I wasn't sure why Cleveland would bring in Rogers instead of a lefty to face Alvarez, and given Alvarez's streakiness, it felt like the Indians were serving a three-run homer on a platter. Sure enough, Rogers threw a knee-high fastball inside, and Alvarez smacked it for probably the most predictable homer a Pirate had hit in the past decade.

The offense, so absent in the early days of the season, was now not only present but downright great. Coupled with a capable pitching staff, it now looked like the Pirates might stay in contention, at least for a while. An upcoming series against a very weak Twins pitching staff certainly helped, as the Bucs scored seven runs in the series opener and nine in the finale to take two of three.

In fact, beginning with the Indians series in mid-June, the Bucs didn't lose another series for a month. After the Twins, the Bucs held their own against the Tigers and Phillies before heading to sweltering St. Louis. In the first game against the Cardinals – a night game that was 101 degrees at first pitch – the Bucs hit four homers in a 14-5 rout. In the second Cards matchup, Alvarez's first-inning grand slam off Lance Lynn keyed a 7-3 victory. The Bucs dropped the last game of the series, but by they were still 42-36 with a four-game set against Houston on the horizon.

Ah, the Astros. Houston was set for a move to the American League, but first the Astros would play the Pirates 17 times in 2012. And how lucky for the Pirates that they did, because the Astros, like the Cubs, were like ghosts of Pirates teams past. The Astros continued to trot out lineups full of players most fans had never heard of – I was thrilled with myself one day when I looked at a tweet of their lineup and figured out all the batters' first names without having to look anyone up. And their bullpen churned through pitchers who were not only anonymous, but who didn't even sound *real*, as if their names had been created by some bored *Major League Baseball 2K14* programmer to fill out the player universe on franchise mode. Chuckie Fick. Rhiner Cruz. Xavier Cedeno. Mickey Storey.

The Pirates won the first game in an 11-2 blowout in which Garrett Jones and Neil Walker hit back-to-back home runs that, improbably, *both* clanked off the right-field foul pole. But it was the second game that Bucs fans would remember.

The Bucs came back in the middle innings after A.J. Burnett's rough start. Andrew McCutchen hit a two-run homer in the fourth, and Pedro Alvarez keyed a big sixth inning with a two-run single. Jones' two-run shot gave the Pirates the lead in the seventh. Joel Hanrahan entered in the ninth up 7-6, but blew the save when he walked Jed Lowrie and allowed a double to Jason Castro.

But in the Pirates' half of the inning, Drew Sutton, a journeyman who had already gone from the Braves to the Pirates to the Rays and back to the Pirates in the 2012 season, came up with one out and took a called strike from Wesley Wright, then a ball. Wright then threw a curveball outside, and Sutton hit it hard to dead center. It cleared the fence for a walk-off win, and Sutton rounded first raising his arms and shouting in obvious joy. It felt like a microcosm of the season as a whole – here was a player who had spent an eternity on the periphery of the majors, and now here he was at the center of it all. Meanwhile, the Pirates, after nearly two decades of irrelevance, were beginning to attract attention. And, more importantly, they'd tied the Reds for first place in the NL Central.

The Pirates kept winning. They beat the Astros again the next day 6-4, and the Reds lost, leaving the Pirates alone atop the division. The Bucs then completed the sweep, getting eight shutout innings from Jeff Karstens, and moved to 10 games over .500. After taking two of three against the Giants and scoring 13 runs against Tim Lincecum and the San Francisco bullpen in the series finale, the Bucs headed into the All-Star break at 48-37. They had also scored 32 more runs than they had allowed at that point, suggesting that their record wasn't a complete fluke.

A peculiar hand sign, in which players put the tips of their thumbs together and turned their palms opposite one another to form a "Z" shape, came to symbolize the Pirates' run at contention. The Z stood for "Zoltan," a reference to the movie *Dude, Where's My Car?* "It was just so terrible and stupid," Neil Walker told the *Post-Gazette*. "We just pulled that from it. It's just kind of our team way of bonding, I guess." Fans caught on, frequently wearing black-and-gold "Z" shirts to the ballpark.

The Bucs headed to Milwaukee after the break and quickly found themselves in a high-scoring opening game, thanks to James McDonald's poor performance. The two teams were tied 6-6 in the eighth when Clint Hurdle sent lefty Tony Watson to face former Pirate Nyjer Morgan. The Brewers replaced Morgan with righty Carlos Gomez, who popped out. Despite having a fresh bullpen at his disposal, though, Hurdle hung Watson out to dry against the all-righty heart of the Milwaukee order. Ryan Braun and Aramis Ramirez each singled. Watson struck out Corey Hart, but Braun stole third and Ramirez stole second, and Watson intentionally walked Rickie Weeks. And then light-hitting Cody Ransom – also a righty – blasted a waist-high fastball for a grand slam. The Pirates lost 10-7.

It was an annoying loss, made all the more annoying by the fact that Jason Grilli, the Pirates' best reliever in 2012 *and a righty*,

Dry Land

never made it into the game. But the Pirates were still 10 games over .500, and in a long season, these things happen, right?

Ultimately, that wasn't how some Pirates fans took it. Many were furious with Hurdle and concerned for McDonald, whose brilliant pitching in the first half had been a key to the Pirates' surprissurprising start.

"Looks like a disaster," one wrote. "Can anything go right anymore ever again?"

Welcome to life as a Pirates fan. You're 10 games above .500, and yet any loss looks like the beginning of the end.

It wasn't. At least not yet. The Bucs took one of the two remaining games from the Brewers, then won two of three against a struggling Rockies team. More bad teams followed, and after series against the Marlins, Cubs, Astros, and Cubs again, the Bucs found themselves 16 games above .500.

Nonetheless, the quality of their play had diminished. The Astros series was a case in point. The Astros' losses in the first three of the four games of the series were their 10th, 11th and 12th in a row. In the second game, the Bucs needed two ninth-inning walks, and then scored the go-ahead run on a wild pitch by Xavier Cedeno. In the third game, the Pirates faced Armando Galarraga, who was making his first big-league start in over a year. He struck out five Bucs and walked just one. The Pirates tied the game at three in the sixth, thanks to an Astros error and passed ball, before Rod Barajas knocked in the go-ahead run with a single in the eighth. Then, the Pirates lost the last game of the series as McDonald walked seven batters.

In other words, the Pirates had won three out of four, but this was not an impressive series. They hadn't won games so much as an awful Astros team had lost them. And the series ended with McDonald, one of the keys to the Pirates' first half, coming apart.

The Pirates were very much in the playoff hunt, and when you're in the hunt in late July, you've got a chance. In spite of that, there were signs that the Bucs might not be able to keep it together much longer.

As the trade deadline approached, Pirates fans were on tenterhooks, not only because of the perception that the Bucs were at least one really good player from being in playoff shape, but because many Pirates fans treat every opportunity to spend on veterans as a test for the team's ownership. Never mind that committing too heavily to veterans, either by trading good prospects to get them or by agreeing to multiyear contracts, can hamstring a smaller-payroll team for years to come. There's a reason that, for example, the successful Tampa Bay Rays aren't generally big players at the trade deadline. The impact of a single player on a team's drive toward contention is often minimal, and acquiring a star is typically costly.

Most Pirates fans, and many of the commentators whose opinions guide them, were uninterested in that sort of calculus, instead treating the trade deadline as an excuse to beat their chests. "The Pirates need to get a bat by the deadline today, or management will have let this team down," Dejan Kovacevic wrote, pointing to the standings as evidence. "Chances like this *cannot* be wasted. Not now, not ever. No excuses. Get it done."

That sort of silliness was typical of the discussion at the time. For a general manager, there are few absolutes, and proceeding as if you *must* do something is a sure way to get yourself into trouble. When you trade veterans, you're deliberately tanking in the hopes of a future reward. That's straightforward enough. But when you're *acquiring* them, you're sacrificing future value, *even though you still want to win in the future*, in order to win in the present. Any team that considers itself a buyer in the trade market is, by definition, juggling competing goals.

On top of that, a GM who wants to be a buyer has to balance his concerns against the market. If you want to acquire Bartolo Colon, and the team you're trading with wants Cliff Lee, Brandon Phillips and Grady Sizemore, you say no. It doesn't matter if, ideally, you would acquire Bartolo Colon. A smart GM won't acquire a star hitter because he has to. He'll acquire a star hitter because it's the right deal.

Dry Land

Neal Huntington's performance at the trade deadline wasn't perfect, but it showed he understood the need to upgrade the team without sacrificing its future. Huntington's first move, and his biggest, was to acquire Wandy Rodriguez from the Astros for prospects Robbie Grossman, Rudy Owens and Colton Cain. Grossman had a chance to be a solid regular, but his most likely career outcome was that of a fourth outfielder. Neither Owens nor Cain figured to bite the Pirates too badly. Rodriguez replaced the mediocre Kevin Correia in the rotation, and he provided the Bucs with insurance in case McDonald or another pitcher struggled. The Pirates would also control Rodriguez's rights in 2013, meaning that the trade wasn't purely a rental.

Huntington didn't get much credit for the deal, probably because the pitching was widely perceived to be a team strength, but Rodriguez was a minor star in Houston (the Astros were a horrible team, but it's still worth noting that Rodriguez graced the cover of their media guide), and he was useful to the Pirates, who needed pitching help as well as offense. Rodriguez became one of the few reliable Bucs players as the team struggled down the stretch.

"I really liked the trade," Todd says. "[It was] just like I looked at the A.J. Burnett deal. They're getting a guy who, yeah, he's a little bit older, but they've got him under control for a period of time, and he's going to be a stabilizing force in this rotation."

If the reaction to the Rodriguez trade was muted, though, most fans' takes on the rest of Huntington's trades before the deadline were downright negative. His swap of reliever Brad Lincoln for Blue Jays outfielder Travis Snider was greeted with confusion. The trade aimed to accomplish several goals at once, whereas many fans would have preferred an unambiguous prospects-for-veteran deal for a name hitter like Chase Headley (who would have worked out brilliantly, at least down the stretch in 2012) or Shane Victorino or Hunter Pence (who would not have).

Nevertheless, there was hope that Snider would immediately step into the Pirates outfield alongside Starling Marte and Andrew McCutchen and provide power and decent defense. Also, the Bucs would control him for years to come, and at 24, he might improve. In practice, though, the deal didn't work out, at least not in 2012, as Snider struggled with hamstring problems. (As it turned out, Snider didn't hit much in 2013, either.)

The Bucs' other two deals were puzzling. They shipped outfielder Gorkys Hernandez and a competitive-balance draft pick to the Marlins for first baseman Gaby Sanchez and a minor-leaguer. Sanchez was in the midst of an awful year, and it looked like his main use to the Pirates would be as a right-handed platoon partner to Garrett Jones at first base. The Pirates already had a player like that in Casey McGehee. So with their next deal, they shipped McGehee to the Yankees for reliever Chad Qualls. Qualls hadn't pitched well since 2009, so it appeared the Pirates were mostly just trying to find another team for McGehee, for whom they no longer had any use.

In any case, the Rodriguez and Snider deals were the main ones, and they made plenty of sense. Snider didn't end up hitting, but Rodriguez was a reliable arm in a rotation that, as it turned out, would badly need one.

In August, the Pirates' performance began to slow before it came to a halt in September. The Bucs won their first game in August, against the Cubs, but dropped the first two games of their next series against a red-hot Cincinnati team. In the first of those two games, Mat Latos, Jonathan Broxton and Aroldis Chapman four-hit the Bucs, and the game turned ugly in the ninth, when Chapman hit McCutchen with a 100-MPH fastball. The Pirates won the following game, but they were still 4.5 games back in the NL Central, and in a tough spot.

It didn't get better. The Bucs began a disappointing homestand against NL West teams – they took two of four from the Diamondbacks, but went 1-2 against the Padres and 1-3 against the Dodgers. They took two of three against the Cardinals, then suffered more pain against the NL West, as the Padres swept them. Then they lost a series against the Brewers, falling to 68-59 in the process.

Dry Land

The Bucs again took two of three from the Cardinals, the only team they seemed to be able to beat at the time, and also the only team keeping the Pirates within spitting distance of the playoffs. The Cardinals might have bounced the Pirates out of the race if they'd taken down their two August series with the Bucs, but the Pirates won both to remain in the hunt for the second Wild Card spot. After a predictable sweep at the hands of the Brewers in Miller Park, the Bucs took two of three against the Astros, then got swept yet again, this time by the lowly Cubs. Somehow, even as the Pirates fell to just five games above .500, they remained in the race, as the Cardinals struggled to string together wins.

Thinking about things that way seemed increasingly counterintuitive, however. "There are more than three weeks of baseball left. They have a chance. Nothing is inevitable," I wrote in September, reasoning that the ups and downs in a season could be difficult to predict, and if the Pirates seemed to be falling apart, it didn't need to continue that way. They were still just two games out of a playoff spot.

Some Bucs Dugout readers reacted viscerally to my argument. "Technically," went one ultra-glib response. "Is this a joke?" went another. Intellectually, I disagreed, but emotionally, I was right there with them. The math said the Pirates still had a shot at the playoffs, but it certainly didn't feel like it. Following the Bucs became increasingly excruciating, as a playoff spot slipped away, gradually but seemingly inevitably.

The Pirates' play the rest of the season strongly suggested the doubters had been right. The Bucs didn't win another series until the last one of the year, foundering as the Reds and Brewers swept them, and even losing their last series against the Astros. They fell all the way back to .500 on September 19, then kept falling, ultimately finishing at 79-83.

As with 2011, analyzing the Pirates' decline seemed ridiculous. It felt like the team had merely been blown out to sea by the winds of fate. Fundamentally, their decline wasn't about statistics, or the performance of specific players. It was just the universe messing with us.

But what the heck: James McDonald posted a 7.52 ERA in the second half. Erik Bedard got poor results in seven second-half starts before being released. Andrew McCutchen, in the midst of an MVP-caliber season through July, posted a .693 OPS in August. As McCutchen returned to normal in September, the rest of the offense vanished. The Pirates scored 100 runs in September – down from 146 in June and 130 in July – and allowed 142. They went 7-21 that month.

As the Pirates limped to the finish line, they lost series to the Mets and Reds. One of those Reds losses was a no-hitter by Homer Bailey. The no-hitter itself felt oddly inconsequential, but the loss was the Pirates' 81st of the season, ruling out the possibility of a winning record. It would have felt strange to celebrate an 82-win season at that point, but at least the streak would have been over. The Bucs ended by taking two of three from the Braves in a series that was meaningless to them. They dropped the last game.

For the few fans still paying attention, these last few weeks were rough. "I kept watching and listening until the bitter end, but the games hurt," writes Bucs Dugout contributor John Fredland. "I was crushed."

"Back in July I was looking at ticket prices to fly in to Pittsburgh in order to see what I thought would be a huge game before the playoffs," one Bucs Dugout commenter wrote, ruefully.

In general, though, most fans simply drifted away, turning their attention to the Steelers or to school or something else. As the possibility of a 20th straight losing season appeared ever more likely, there wasn't much gnashing of teeth over the Pirates' failure to break the streak – not because it didn't hurt, but because fans had already been so thoroughly disappointed. In reality, the season had ended weeks before, and many fans had temporarily exhausted their supply of despair. While the Pirates had once again provided a few months of excitement, the disappointment over another losing year lingered through the offseason. The Bucs' streak was now two decades old. In another year it would be old enough to legally drink. And the Pirates' long stretch of winning, followed by two months of losing, had their fans feeling duped.

"I was pissed at myself for how much time I put into sports via the Pirates after the poor outcome," wrote a Bucs Dugout reader.

"I became a fan in the mid-90s, so I've never known a winning team, and I've never given up on the Pirates, in the sense of no longer listening to or attending games. But [in 2012] I did," wrote another.

The collapse didn't leave *all* Pirates fans feeling broken. "I was still pleased with the progress they'd made compared to the prior season," wrote Vlad, a Bucs Dugout author. "If there's one thing I've learned over the years as a Pirates fan, it's how to be philosophical about losing games."

Chapter 9

The Pirates had their first winning season in two decades well within their grasp, and they dropped it, leaving behind broken pieces of what-ifs. Not the kinds of what-ifs a fan of another team might entertain – even at the height of the 2012 season, few Bucs fans considered the Pirates World Series contenders. But they had reason to hope the Bucs would break the streak, at least.

The Pirates weren't the only perennial loser to flirt with contention in 2012. The Baltimore Orioles had 14 straight losing years before pulling off an unlikely 93-win season, and capturing a playoff berth, in 2012. Shortly after that 2012 season, I spoke to Sam Dingman of the brilliant Orioles podcast Baltimorons, which he and a friend had founded earlier that year as a way of coping with what he thought would be another bad team. Dingman was still reeling from the Orioles' elimination from the playoffs.

"The feeling for me is very much like I have just been thrown very abruptly off a roller coaster," he says.

Like the Pirates' never-ending streak, the Orioles' era of losing was so long, it could be measured in life-defining events.

"My parents got divorced when I was older, when I was 20. I was talking to my mom this year, and she was saying, 'I'm really starting to realize that I've come a long way, and that our family has come a long way,'" he says.

Dry Land

"I, of course, instantly went to thinking about baseball, and was like, 'My entire family has fallen apart and rebuilt itself in a shorter time than since the Orioles last won 82 games.'"

The Orioles' playoff run introduced Dingman to a whole new kind of fandom, one that Pirates fans hadn't truly experienced in two decades.

"I invest so much of my emotions and so much of my time every year, but I think I have always done a very good job of keeping it in the proper context, as it relates to the rest of my life," he says. "I hadn't turned girlfriends into baseball widows." The fact that the Orioles were consistently below average allowed Dingman to root for them with a sense of detachment.

In an earlier chat, Dingman had told me that he connected the Orioles' disappointing run to his own struggles and confusions with young adulthood – things weren't quite turning out the way he had imagined, but through it all, both he and the Orioles were at least surviving, and he could dream that one day, things might be different. He was careful about how much of himself he invested in a team that never won.

But all that changed in 2012. "It crossed over from the category of being somewhat escapist, into something I obsessed about more than my professional relevance and well-being, or my personal health," he says.

"It was like, 'If I don't get home in time to watch the game, then I'm going to miss something, and then I'm going to have severed this connection that's kept me going for so long.' And so, instead of being a stress-*reliever*, it became a stress-*inducer*."

Down the stretch, Dingman fought off his newfound stress by burrowing even further into Orioles fandom, watching five or more games a week instead of his usual two or three. Right before paying for an expensive vacation, he bought tickets to Orioles playoff games, then realized he wasn't quite sure how to pay for everything.

"When they switched over to being a team that the rest of baseball was going to take seriously, I had to take it *even more* seriously," he says.

Dingman found himself glued to the games as never before, watching with bated breath until the final out and then switching the channel to see what the rival Yankees were doing. He compares the experience to jazz, which the listener can appreciate on a superficial level or as something much more complex, even nearly all-consuming. He began planning his life around the Orioles in a way he'd never previously thought to.

"This vacation that I had planned was in mid-October," he says. "In June, when we planned it, it didn't even occur to me that there would be a reason to not go on vacation in October. ... I'm in a country with no internet connection for Games 4 and 5 of the American League Division Series." He suddenly understood why his friend, a Yankees fan, became so unreliable in the fall.

"Now I get it," he says. "It's like a higher calling than I'm accustomed to."

I ask how he would be affected if the Orioles went back to their usual ways in 2013. (As it turned out, they won 85 games, although they missed the playoffs.)

"If they regress terribly next season, I'm going to be crushed, but I know that I'm not going to stop loving them," he says.

> This season has validated the part of myself that stubbornly believed against all belief that there *was* a winning team out there on that field, despite all the indicators to the contrary. And so, even if I have to reduce myself to doing it on a game-by-game basis, I'm going to know that, on any given night, the Orioles could go out and beat the team in the other dugout. [Everything] feels so much richer because we went through the hell and didn't give up. So when things get bad, it's not going to feel as bleak this time, because if nothing else, we now have proof that, periodically,

the cosmic narrative does turn around, and when that happens, it feels good enough. It's worth 15 years, if that's what it takes.

The Orioles' surprising 2012 season affected not only Dingman himself, but people who spent time with him who normally weren't nearly as emotionally invested in the Orioles' success but who ended up watching games with him over the summer.

"They would say things to me like, 'I never realized how much you have gone through, and how good this must feel,'" he says. He remembers a friend telling him, "It makes you feel good for being loyal to something and committing to something. It validates this part of your history that a lot of people had written off."

Orioles fans aren't the only ones who were in the same boat with fans of the Pirates. Northeast Ohio native Scott McCauley has been through the worst with his hometown Cleveland Browns. So, as the broadcaster for the Indianapolis Indians, the Pirates' Triple-A team, from 2006 through 2011, he understood where Bucs fans were coming from.

"I talk to other announcers around the [Triple-A International League]," he says, describing in great detail the extent to which Pirates fans scour minor-league box scores. "The way that [Pirates fans] follow the minor-leaguers, I've never seen anything like it for any other team."

I ask him why he thinks Pirates fans follow the minor leagues so closely.

"20 years of losing is going to do that," he says. "Once Littlefield left, I feel like there was some kind of sense of, 'Maybe these first-rounders will now pan out.'"

He points to the Pirates' selection of Pedro Alvarez in 2008, and the development of Andrew McCutchen at around that time, as reasons Bucs fans suddenly became fixated on the minor leagues. I suggest that, also, the inattention to the farm system under Littlefield demonstrated to serious fans how important minor-leaguers actually were.

"You're right," he tells me for a Bucs Dugout interview. "Remember in '08, all four of those guys in the Yankees deal [Jose Tabata, Jeff Karstens, Ross Ohlendorf and Daniel McCutchen, who were acquired for Xavier Nady and Damaso Marte] made it to the big leagues, but the big key was, those were three arms in Triple-A, and that didn't exist."

McCauley also notes the rise of blogs and Twitter as other key reasons Pirates fans began following the minor leagues in large numbers. The independent website Pirates Prospects, which began covering the Bucs' farm system in great detail, pushed many fans in that direction, and so did the availability of live minor-league box scores.

Whatever the reasons, McCauley was amazed by Pirates fans' interest in their team's minor-leaguers, an interest he knew was connected to the team's losing streak at the major-league level. And he knew where the fans were coming from, because of his own rooting interest in the Browns.

McCauley made the connection between the two franchises in a heartfelt essay on his blog in 2012. It was a connection that neither fan base had explored much, in part because Pittsburgh sports fans aren't usually particularly interested in empathizing with Clevelanders, and vice versa. (Even McCauley says of Pittsburgh, "I love that city. It pains me to say that.") But it was a powerful connection nonetheless.

"It amazed me how many people outside of Indy were interested in the [Indianapolis] Indians," he wrote. "Sometimes I felt like the fans in Pittsburgh cared more about the players than the fans in Indy. ... Maybe I can relate to Pirates fans because they remind me of Browns fans. Even with all the losing and all the moments when it looks like there is no hope, you remember your roots and stick with the club through thick and thin."

Later, I ask him when he last felt that being a Browns fan was doing him any good, and he says 2002. For the last game of that sea-

Dry Land

son, McCauley went to a sports bar in Indianapolis wearing a Browns jersey, along with a Jets pullover and a Dolphins wind-breaker, hoping for a perfect series of results that would send the Browns to the playoffs. The Browns beat the Falcons, finished 9-7, and did sneak in as the last Wild Card team, only to lose in the first round as they squandered a 17-point lead against Tommy Maddox and the Steelers. The Browns haven't been back to the playoffs since.

Still, McCauley remains a Browns lifer, despite one attempt to change teams. Two years after the Browns left to become the Balti-more Ravens in 1995, the New York Giants drafted the punter Brad Maynard, McCauley's roommate at Ball State. "I jumped on, full-bore," McCauley says. "I joked that we needed to find a fire hydrant [and] hose me down for at least an hour just to get the hate out of my soul."

In his time as a Giants fan, McCauley says, "I treated a lot of the games like [one does] today with Monday Night Football – you watched with no care."

And so it's no surprise that when the Browns returned to Cleveland in 1999, McCauley reverted to his old ways. "I was really excited when they came back, even though they're garbage," he says.

He now watches Browns games in cycles of frustration and hope. "Each Sunday I genuinely believe if they play the perfect game they can beat anybody, even the Steelers," he says. But those optimistic thoughts crash into a brick wall by about the third quar-ter. "Usually by the end of the day Sunday I'm in a pretty bad mood, but I'll be back on board by Thursday," he says.

Like Pirates fans during the streak, McCauley typically gives up on his team well before the end of its season. "By the time Thanksgiving rolls around, I'm watching a lot of college football, because I know that the Browns will be drafting within the first hour," he says. "By December, I'm just playing out the string."

In some respects, following a bad football team is different from following a bad baseball team. Since pro football teams play ten times fewer games than pro baseball teams do, it's possible to hang onto every win and loss without a bad team ruining one's life. And in football, even losing holds immediate hope that the near future might be different, since the right first-round pick can make a quick, dramatic impact on an NFL team. That's not so in baseball.

Of course, that might not *really* be true for the Browns, either. When I interviewed McCauley in 2012, he was talking about how recent first-rounder Brandon Weeden was "accurate" and how, if you looked at the Browns in the right light, you could imagine how they might go 8-8 or 9-7. Whoops. But you can hardly blame McCauley for *trying* to believe.

The MLB team whose history is most similar to the Pirates' is the Kansas City Royals – the two teams were brothers in small-market incompetence for nearly two decades. The Royals had eight straight losing seasons before winning 83 games in 2003. They quickly returned to irrelevance, with nine more losing seasons in a row until 2013, when they broke their streak as the Pirates broke theirs. No fan base in baseball understands the plight of the Pirates fan better than Royals fans do.

"You became apathetic to the losing," says David Hill, who blogs about the Royals at KingsOfKauffman.com. "You just didn't expect anything."

Even the Royals' one winning season during that period was mostly a fluke, and Hill notes that a number of key players from that team (like Aaron Guiel, Ken Harvey, Desi Relaford, Darrell May and Runelvys Hernandez) fell off the face of the earth almost as soon as the season was over. The 2004 Royals acquired a number of cheap veterans to boost themselves to the next level, but most of them didn't help, and the Royals lost 104 games.

"To me, the face of that was Juan Gonzalez," Hill says. The former Rangers slugger signed with Kansas City after missing much of the 2003 with a torn calf muscle. He collected 127 at bats with the Royals, didn't hit much, and ended his career after one more at bat with Cleveland the following season.

Dry Land

"When those signings didn't work, it's almost as if Royals ownership said, 'You know what, this doesn't work, so this is an excuse for us not to [spend money],'" says Hill. The Royals lost at least 100 games in each of the next two years as well, then continued to lose before they finally developed a winning core and won 86 games in 2013.

In the late 1990s and early 2000s, Rob Neyer helped introduce sabermetric ideas to a wide audience as a writer for ESPN.com. On the side, he and Rany Jazayerli wrote occasional articles about the Royals, and posted them on Neyer's website.

"I got more and more discouraged, and more and more negative, about the team as things never seemed to improve," he told me in early 2013. As the losing seasons piled up following the Royals' strange 2003 dalliance with contention, Neyer's passion for the team began to fade.

"I certainly still follow them more than I follow any other team," he says, noting that he'll often watch the Royals if there isn't another game he needs to watch and if they aren't losing. "I've gotten to the point where, if they fall behind in a game, it's very easy for me to change channels. I'm sort of the worst version of the fairweather, fickle fan."

Neyer finds it hard to be hopeful about the current team. He says its general manager, Dayton Moore, is "pretty good at scouting" but doesn't know how to evaluate major-league talent. Moore has drawn fire from the Royals' fan base for his fascination with flawed veterans like Jeff Francoeur and Yuniesky Betancourt, as well as his controversial and potentially destructive trade of top outfield prospect Wil Myers, plus three other prospects, for pitchers James Shields and Wade Davis.

The Royals' ineptitude did not begin with Moore, of course. Before him was Allard Baird, who traded Jermaine Dye for Neifi Perez and shipped off Johnny Damon and Mark Ellis for Angel Berroa, A.J. Hinch and Roberto Hernandez. As incompetent general managers go, Baird wasn't on Dave Littlefield's level, but he was close.

The Royals' financial disadvantages have hurt them, Neyer says. But teams as bad as the Royals and Pirates were clearly also deserve their share of the blame. "Only the Royals and the Pirates have gone for as long as those clubs have gone without being competitive," he notes.

He also thinks both teams have been unlucky, in that even a poorly-run franchise ought to back into an 85-win season once in a while.

"You look at the teams that have gone to the playoffs while being outscored – it doesn't happen often, but it does happen," he says.

"You could also look at prospects not panning out. ... All it takes is two or three prospects not panning out, high draft picks, to really screw up three or four years," he adds. "If you develop two great young players, it can make your team look completely different, and there's a lot of luck involved there."

Baseball fans love to warn each other against rushing to judgment on small sample sizes – a strong 100 at-bat start to a season might be the beginning of a breakout for a young player, but it might also simply be chance. But fans rarely apply that logic to the development of prospects, even though that's also a sample-size issue. The Pirates' losing streak was bleak, and their player development was abysmal during most of it. But if only Chad Hermansen and J.R. House and Bobby Bradley and Bryan Bullington had turned out to be good players, the picture might have looked very different. The same is true of the Royals and, say, Mike Stodolka and Chris Lubanski. If just a few more top draft picks had turned out well, the Pirates and Royals might have merely been mediocre franchises dealt a bad hand from MLB's stacked deck, rather than teams in the midst of losing streaks of a decade or more. That there's a difference might seem depressing, but it's significant.

Even leaving aside the matter of luck with prospects (which some Pirates fans might not find particularly compelling anyway, given that the Bucs' ineptitude clearly played a role in their prospects' struggles), posting 20 straight losing seasons is *difficult*. Dave

Dry Land

Cameron of FanGraphs.com points out that predicting a team's record in any given season is much tougher than most of us imagine. Even if we knew exactly what each team's true talent level was, and we could accurately predict the number of singles, doubles, walks and so on that they would accumulate and allow in a given season (which is impossible, for more reasons than we can count here), we should expect a broad distribution of runs scored for teams with the same number of hits, walks and so on. Some hits and walks lead to runs, while others don't.

And even if we knew how many runs a team would score and allow, we couldn't comfortably predict how many games they would win, at least not in a sample size as small as 162 games. The 2012 Orioles, for example, won 11 more games than their Pythagorean record (a shorthand for the won-loss record we should expect based on a team's runs scored and runs allowed) suggested they would. Even a team that ought to win 70 games will occasionally win 82, and that's even before taking into account possibilities like having players who unexpectedly break out, or having extremely good luck with injuries.

Not even the best teams from the Pirates' losing streak – in particular the 1997, 1999, 2003 and 2012 versions – were actually *good*, and no one of them deserved a winning record. But given how difficult it is to accurately predict how many games a team will win, it's unlucky that *none* of the 20 consecutive losing Pirates teams managed to overcome their lack of talent and string together 82 wins.

Neyer's description of his Royals fandom was familiar to me from following the Pirates when Dave Littlefield in charge. The Bucs weren't a contending team, and I didn't see any hope that they could eventually become one, so rooting for them to win seemed pointless. Instead, I'd root for my favorite players to succeed, while simultaneously rooting for my least favorites to fail. I also enjoyed watching the Pirates' best players, like Brian Giles, Jason Kendall and Jason Bay.

"What I you think you learn to do, if you don't want to go insane, is take whatever small pleasures there are, and enjoy those," Neyer says, mentioning the play of former Royals stars Zack Greinke and Mike Sweeney in particular.

However bad a baseball team might be, there are always these small joys, and unexpected turns of events. Even a terrible team can have a winning streak. Even a great one will occasionally get swept. On a day-to-day level, it's unpredictable. And because the season is so long, the result of any one game is easy to shrug off. Most baseball games just aren't that important, regardless of how good the team is. For Pirates fans during the streak, that was a blessing.

Misery loves company. And while the Pirates' losing streak was longer than that of any other major pro team, they did at least have a few other teams in the muck with them. In June 2006, when the Pirates were 26-45 and the Royals 19-49, the Bucs traveled to Kansas City for a three-game set. In an ironic gesture, Pat Lackey live-blogged the first game, relishing every bit of awful baseball. In the midst of a disastrous fourth inning that featured a passed ball, several botched double-play opportunities, and a bases-loaded walk, Lackey wrote, "Coming into this game I expected the ugliest game ever, and this thing is delivering." The Royals ended up winning. But Lackey's sense of the grotesquerie unfolding in front of him was spot-on, and it probably was as clear from Kansas City as it had been from Pittsburgh.

Chapter 10

In 1992, Mike LaValliere caught Barry Bonds' throw as Sid Bream scored the Braves' winning run in Game 7 of the NLCS. The play that ended the Pirates' season also ended an era in Pittsburgh, as the Pirates lost Bonds that offseason and vanished into the woods. LaValliere went on to play just one more game with the Pirates before being released.

In 2012, the Braves depicted LaValliere's role in the beginning of the Pirates' streak with a bobblehead doll of Bream sliding past his tag. The following spring, a group of former Pirates met at McKechnie Field in Bradenton, placed one of the bobbleheads on home plate, and read a poem. And then LaValliere picked up a sledgehammer and smashed the bobblehead to smithereens. And lo, the Pirates' fortunes began to change.

"I don't believe in witchcraft or any craziness like that," La-Valliere told MLB.com. Regardless, he must have spent the 2013 season wondering if there was some curse out there his act of violence had finally broken.

You know the saying: Fool me once, shame on me. Fool me twice ... well, actually, Pirates fans *did* get fooled twice. But they weren't eager to be fooled a third time.

The 2012 collapse had been particularly difficult for Pirates fans to swallow. For the second straight year, the Pirates had fallen apart, not only adding another losing season to the column but also demonstrating yet again that four full months of winning baseball could be a lie. 2012 was particularly cruel, because Pirates fans thought they had learned that lesson already, in 2011, and here came the 2012 team, playing better than the 2011 team ever had and looking like a more legitimate contender. And yet, in the end, the 2012 team was just another disappointment.

The 2012-13 offseason was relatively quiet, or at least that's how it seemed at the time. The Pirates' biggest move was to sign Russell Martin to a two-year contract to be their starting catcher. The deal didn't excite Pirates fans much, since Martin's offensive numbers were pedestrian. But given his defensive reputation and his ability to frame pitches (not to mention the wretched performance of the player he replaced, Rod Barajas), Martin stood a chance of making an impact.

The Bucs also signed starting pitcher Francisco Liriano, adjusting the terms of his contract after he broke his non-pitching arm in an offseason accident at his home. Liriano had mostly frustrated his previous employers, but his stuff and strikeout rate gave him upside. He also stood to benefit from a move to PNC Park, which is friendly to lefty pitchers, and to the National League. Given Liriano's inconsistency in previous seasons, there was every possibility that the move would blow up in Neal Huntington's face, and it was to Huntington's credit that he was willing to gamble, even after two straight collapses.

The Pirates' other big move was their least popular – they traded closer Joel Hanrahan (who would make about $7 million in his final year before free-agent eligibility) and infielder Brock Holt to the Red Sox for four players. One of them, reliever Mark Melancon, would play a prominent role with the Pirates in 2013. Hanrahan's walk rate had ballooned in 2012, and Melancon, whose abilities to get strikeouts and ground balls suggested he would bounce back from a tough season, looked like he would at least be an adequate replacement. And trying to get *something* for Hanrahan, an aging closer who would soon hit free agency, was the right move on the

Pirates' part. But it was easy to understand fans' frustration at the departure of a popular player.

The Pirates appeared to have modestly upgraded their roster, and they also figured to benefit from full seasons of Wandy Rodriguez and perhaps also Travis Snider, both of whom they had acquired at the previous year's trade deadline. But the Bucs' offseason transactions hadn't obviously represented a grand leap forward, and despite a talent level that appeared slightly higher, they would have to fight an uphill battle to improve on their 79-83 2012 record, given the departure of the woeful Astros from the NL Central to the AL West. If the Bucs were going to take a step forward, they would likely need big seasons from young outfielders Andrew McCutchen and Starling Marte. And the Pirates' rotation, riddled with question marks, would have to hold up.

On paper, the 2013 Pirates looked like the best Bucs team in at least a decade. And yet they still didn't appear particularly promising – an 82-win season wouldn't be impossible, but it would be difficult. And though their semi-respectable final record in 2012 had reduced fans' anger at Huntington, there was still the sense that he'd had more than enough time to turn the franchise around. A late-2012 pseudo-scandal involving the Pirates' use of military-style training techniques didn't help his reputation, either.

And so the Pirates began the 2013 season at a crossroads. If they had a poor season, Huntington and Frank Coonelly would likely be fired. If they finished above .500, there would be no chance of that. The 2013 team looked like it might fall somewhere in the middle of those two outcomes.

As a result, as spring training began, Bucs fans were happy for the arrival of baseball season, but they ranged from wary to moderately optimistic about the team. At least they weren't feeling abjectly miserable, but then, there's no better time for optimism to grow than in the spring, and yet the optimism trees weren't exactly thriving.

Dry Land

"I feel like a man who's been married to the Pirates for 40 years," one Bucs Dugout commenter wrote. "The 'relations' still happen, and they're nice, but I just can't get that excited anymore."

"After last year's collapse, [I] did some soul-searching and asked if I wanted to continue to commit emotionally to this franchise," wrote another. "I guess I'm in it for life, regardless of how many consecutive losing seasons. Rooting for a shitty team is better than not having a team at all."

Beginnings of seasons are always strange. A stretch of five games tells us very little about a baseball team. And yet, when the season is five games old, we only have five games' worth of tea leaves, and we cannot help but to try to read them. When the Pirates win, we feel invincible. When they lose, we feel awful.

The Pirates lost five of their first six games in 2013, producing just eight runs total. They were two-hit twice by the Dodgers, and three-hit by the Cubs.

Echoes of the Bucs offense's slow 2012 start reverberated throughout the fan base. It looked possible that the Bucs' bats might take April and May off yet again. But the Pirates started hitting earlier in 2013 than they had in 2012. They won a series in Arizona (with their hitters getting to Trevor Cahill and Brandon McCarthy in the first two games), then took three in a row from the Reds, the last of which was a thrilling come-from-behind win.

Starter Phil Irwin, making his big-league debut, coughed up four runs in the early innings, but Michael McKenry led off the seventh with a homer to center off Mat Latos, and the Bucs followed with three two-out runs that inning to cut the lead to one. Then, in the eighth, after Jared Hughes allowed a run to make it 6-4, Pedro Alvarez led off with a walk, and McKenry belted a fly ball that just cleared the wall in left, tying the game at six. Jose Tabata walked two batters later and came home when Starling Marte followed with a homer of his own, and the Pirates were off to the races.

When the dust settled, the Pirates had won 10-7 and they were back at .500. Then they didn't lose another series until the end of the month, and after a 9-0 thrashing of the Cardinals on April 28, the Bucs were alone in first place with a 15-10 record.

In the wake of the two previous collapses, the fan base was nonplussed by the Pirates' strong April. On 93.7 The Fan, Colin Dunlap explained why, speaking for any number of fans who felt the same way.

> Until I see that 27th out caught in that 82nd victory, I just can't get all that excited, especially after what happened last year. Everybody in this town was talking, when they were 16 games above .500, talking about NLCS tickets. ... I just can't go there until it really happens, because for me, my 20-something years have been filled with failure after failure after failure after failure. I can't hope anymore. I've got to see the proof.

I understood where Dunlap was coming from. If the universe was playing a joke on us in 2011 and 2012, there was no reason it couldn't play an even worse one in 2013. But it seemed like a shame. The Pirates' hot start offered fans an opportunity to put aside their negativity – toward the streak, toward the GM, toward each other – and enjoy genuinely good baseball. While the negativity *did* die down somewhat in late April and early May, not much enthusiasm replaced it.

It was the bad-weather portion of the season, of course, and the Penguins were making a playoff run. But while some fans slumbered, they were missing an exciting team. Starling Marte appeared to be emerging as one of the game's top young outfielders, thanks in part to his excellent defense in PNC's big left field. Six weeks into the season, A.J. Burnett led the National League in strikeouts. Jason Grilli took well to the closer job, and Mark Melancon looked dominant as his setup man. Russell Martin dramatically improved the team's defense at catcher, and opposing runners no longer stole bases at will. And Andrew McCutchen was just beginning to warm up after a relatively slow start. Simply put, the Pirates didn't look like a joke. They weren't backing into wins the way the 2011 team had sometimes seemed to.

Another team's GM told FOX Sports' Ken Rosenthal that the 2013 Pirates were the best Bucs team he'd seen since 1992. Adding a punch line was easy, of course. But that GM appeared to be right. And yet the beginning of the Bucs' season felt like a tree falling that few were around to hear.

Rooting in a conflicted way is part of being a Pirates fan. Years earlier, I had believed that the Bucs would never have sustained success as long as Dave Littlefield was in charge, and so it had been impossible for me to root, unambiguously, for the Pirates to win each game, even though, ultimately, winning mattered deeply to me.

And yet, in this case, Pirates fans' conflicted nature seemed unfortunate. If we had to wait for the Pirates' 82nd win to get excited, then from how many seasons, and how much baseball, would we keep our distance? And with any reasonable answer to those questions beginning with "many" or "a lot," what was the point in being Pirates fans at all? If the 2013 team was playing genuinely good baseball, shouldn't we just enjoy it? And when the Pirates finally had a winning season – whenever that might be – wouldn't we appreciate it more when they finally *did* get that 82nd win?

"You get called a cynic, or whatever," Dunlap told me later. "But it's kind of like … if somebody's incessantly late to your home, and they're on schedule to be five minutes early, and they call you, and they're a block from your house, I don't believe it until they walk in my front door."

In May, the Pirates showed few signs of stopping. Francisco Liriano made his season debut May 11 and began pitching brilliantly, joining Burnett atop the Pirates' rotation. In the middle of the month, the Pirates improved to 22-17 after McCutchen hit a walk-off, 12th-inning homer against the Brewers, and they only got better from there.

Charlie Wilmoth

I visited PNC Park about a week later, as the Pirates were wrapping up a sweep of the Cubs to improve to 29-18. Outside the ballpark, the Pirates hung huge banners, each featuring a current player. In past seasons, these banners had been jokes, because the Bucs typically had just three or four genuinely good, banner-worthy players sprinkled among 21 or 22 average or bad ones. You would walk around the stadium and wonder if the world really needed a 12-foot banner dedicated to Ronny Paulino, or Jose Castillo, or Chris Duffy.

This time, I saw players worthy of banners. There would be six or seven banners in a row of players whose performances had been good or downright terrific. And in another new development, many of these players were excelling in part because of strong performances by other players, or because they themselves finally seemed to be in the right roles. Gaby Sanchez hit well because he was well suited to his new role as a lefty-killer, leaving Garrett Jones to start against righties. Clint Barmes gobbled up ground balls for A.J. Burnett, Mark Melancon and several other ground-ball pitchers. Russell Martin's receiving and defense helped nearly all the pitchers improve. And so on. Huntington's offseason additions of Liriano, Melancon and Martin were turning out to be far better than even the most optimistic fans anticipated. The Pirates were more talented than they used to be, but more than that, they appeared to be a team, not just a random collection of players.

Just as the Pens' season appeared to be coming to an end, though, the Pirates started struggling. One weekday night in June, the Penguins lost to fall behind three games to none against the Boston Bruins, and the Pirates were swept and one-hit by the Braves. Wandy Rodriguez left his start early due to forearm tightness, just a few days after Jeanmar Gomez had left a start for the same reason. To me, it simply felt like one of many bumps in the road in a long season, but to many fans, it seemed like the season was ending just as the city began to pay attention.

"It's like we've gone from playing like the Rangers to playing like the Marlins overnight," wrote a Bucs Dugout commenter on

153

Dry Land

June 5. "Everything seems to be falling apart *way* ahead of schedule this year."

But then something strange happened. The injuries to Rodriguez and Gomez prompted the Pirates to promote top prospect Gerrit Cole to join their rotation, and to schedule his first start for June 11. Cole had only recently begun to come around at Triple-A Indianapolis, and his overall numbers there were mediocre – a 2.91 ERA in 68 innings, sure, but with 28 walks and just 47 strikeouts. Neal Huntington told the *Tribune-Review* that the Pirates would have preferred to leave Cole in the minors a little while longer. In this case, though, they didn't have much choice but to promote him.

To a fan base dying for something to make the season seem real, however, that didn't matter. And the timing of Cole's promotion, though incidental, couldn't have been better. Early June is usually peak baseball season in Pittsburgh. *This* June, the Penguins' season had ended, as the Bruins completed the sweep. And Cole's first start coincided with the beginning of a homestand.

Cole debuted before a loud crowd of just over 30,000. He struck out the first batter he faced on three pitches, with the punchout coming on a 99-MPH fastball. The crowd erupted. Cole worked quickly from there, relying heavily on his amazing heater. In the second inning, he came to the plate with two men on and hit an awkward single to right, bringing home two runs. And as the Pirates ran up the score, Cole posted one zero after another before finally running into trouble in the seventh. The Bucs removed him with one out, and the PNC Park crowd couldn't get enough. Here, at least for one night, was a talent that seemed undeniable: a first overall draft pick mowing down hitters with 99-MPH fastballs.

"He keeps the fastball down in the zone," Russell Martin told reporters, including Bucs Dugout's David Manel, after the game. "It just has that heavy feeling when you catch it. ... He's got the best fastball I've ever caught from a starter. There's no question."

Some hardcore fans expressed concern over Cole's overreliance on his fastball, but overall, the fan base was thrilled, noting not only how impressive Cole had been, but what his debut meant in con-

154

text. "Before this year started, I looked toward Cole's debut as an end [in] itself," wrote one Bucs Dugout commenter. "But as this season has progressed, Cole's debut became more than an end. It's a means to an end of competing *now*."

Of course, the Pirates already had their fair share of players capable of doing amazing things – there was Starling Marte with his speed, Pedro Alvarez with his power, Jason Grilli with his strikeouts, Andrew McCutchen with his everything. But Cole conferred at least temporary legitimacy to a team in which fans were having a hard time believing, and he did so at exactly the right time.

The Pirates also seemed to be breaking out of their early-June funk. After being swept by Atlanta, they took two of three from the listless Cubs. And then their offense emerged against the Giants, as they scored eight runs to back Cole in the series opener, and followed that with a 12-8 victory over Barry Zito the next day.

A week later, the Pirates began a streak that finally seemed to wash away some fans' trepidation. They took the finale of a four-game set with the Reds, then swept the Angels, Mariners and Brewers, winning nine in a row. That streak included a spectacular come-from-behind win in which the Pirates scored three runs in the top of the ninth to tie what had been a 6-3 game, then scored four in the tenth and held on, after a last-minute Angels rally, to win 10-9. In the last game of the winning streak, the Bucs' bullpen threw 12 scoreless innings in a 14-inning victory, with Russell Martin sealing the win with a walk-off RBI single. At the season's halfway point, the Bucs had baseball's best record at 51-30, and they were two games up on the Cardinals in the NL Central.

It didn't look like the Pirates could maintain that pace, but they didn't need to. They were a full ten games ahead of the Washington Nationals for the last National League playoff spot. And, with 81 games left, they would finish well above .500 even if they played like a typical 72-win Pirates team the rest of the way. We'd made similar calculations late in the previous summer. But the 2013 team seemed to be playing too well to not be believed.

Dry Land

After shedding their skepticism, fans seemed unsure how to act. "So are we the only fans/media that talk about being so many games over .500, or do all other fans do this too? Say the Cards or Reds?" asked a Bucs Dugout commenter. "Is there a point where we should stop?" TribLIVE Radio host Daniel Dudley briefly started an "#82WinsSucks" hashtag, arguing that Pirates fans should forget about a mere winning season, and aim higher.

Another Bucs Dugout commenter quickly settled the issue. Should the fans stop worrying about being over .500? "Remember, we've gone 20 straight seasons finishing under .500. So no."

"We're also the only fans who will be weeping openly and hugging total strangers when we hit 82," another added.

As skepticism slowly morphed into confidence, some Pirates fans were forced to alter their way of looking at the team. A fan who had spent years wrapping his interest in the team around the supposed incompetence of the front office would surely have been dealing with some cognitive dissonance. In early July, I asked the posters at the Pirates message board Change In Atmosphere how the Bucs' good play had changed their outlook on the team's front office and overall organizational health.

"I do feel better about the organization (which isn't a real high standard for me), but I am still uncertain as to just how much better I feel about it and the future prospects of the franchise with the current regime in charge," said one. He noted that his own aggressive criticism of Neal Huntington before the season had been "pretty overboard," and that Huntington's drafts were beginning to look better than they had before, thanks to productive big-league seasons from Pedro Alvarez, Jordy Mercer and Justin Wilson, and steps forward for prospects Tony Sanchez, Tyler Glasnow, Nick Kingham and Stetson Allie.

Others were less impressed. "My grade for Opie [Huntington] has moved from D- to D+," wrote one.

"I think the majority of people who post here [think] their team was taken hostage by an ownership group that put profits above winning, and that any success must be viewed through the prism of that hostage situation," wrote another.

It wasn't that the "apologists" (a term that suddenly fell out of favor as the Pirates started winning) had reason to gloat, really. Pirates fans had seen the 2011 and 2012 seasons fall apart, so they knew how quickly sweet feelings could turn sour. And much of the Builder outlook was predicated upon taking the long view, rather than overreacting to whether the team was winning or losing at the time.

But, for once, the Pirates' future looked bright. Not only was the team winning, but its farm system looked very strong even after Cole's promotion. Fans still looked for excuses to panic – every two-game losing streak resulted in mentions of a possible collapse. But the Pirates' first winning season in two decades looked very likely, and their long-term health was robust as well.

I found the 2013 season difficult to write about. I could no longer turn to absurdity or moral outrage. And I believed the most likely outcome of the Pirates' season was somewhere between the extremes. The Bucs weren't at all likely to continue at the 102-win pace they'd established through the first 81 games of the season, since a number of Pirates pitchers, Jeff Locke and Jeanmar Gomez chief among them, seemed unlikely to continue piling up zeroes. But unlike the 2011 and 2012 teams, the Bucs seemed to have too much talent to collapse completely.

In late July, the Pirates played a rare five-game series against St. Louis. Five games against the Cardinals, who were perceived before the season to be a likely playoff team and whose run differential was much better than that of the Pirates', represented a significant challenge, and many fans would have would have been satisfied if the Bucs had played competitively and won, say, two of them. Instead, they took the first four games of the series, and won a couple of those in decisive fashion.

Their third matchup – also the second game of a doubleheader – might have been the feel-good game of the season. Spot-starter Brandon Cumpton dominated. The Bucs scored a run on a passed ball in the second. In the fifth, Jordy Mercer hit an RBI single, and then Andrew McCutchen knocked a fly ball toward the short wall in deep left. Matt Holliday drifted back and got in position to catch it, but it caromed off the base of his glove and into the stands.

The ROOT Sports replay lingered luxuriantly as McCutchen's homer left the yard, and just behind Holliday was a young fan-bro reveling in Holliday's mistake, flexing and shouting like he'd just won his frat house's beer pong championship. It was an unbecoming display of the sort you'd associate with fans of the Yankees or Red Sox. And yet it felt right – the Pirates seemed indestructible, and there was nothing to do with this unfamiliar feeling but to bask in it. The Bucs added two more runs in the seventh, won 6-0, and moved into first place that day, again becoming the team with the best record in the majors. And so when, late in the game, they stranded two baserunners who'd each hit leadoff triples, it merely felt like a billionaire giving away a Rolls Royce he didn't need. Who cared? The Pirates were unbeatable.

In contrast with that of the previous season, the 2013 trading deadline came and went quietly. The Pirates needed a right fielder, and Huntington later declared that he'd made offers that had made him feel "incredibly uncomfortable," but in the end, the Pirates were one of many teams that failed to make a significant move. The deadline was quiet throughout baseball, as many non-contending teams declined to sell. At the very least, the Pirates' lack of activity didn't cause them to lose ground – the Cardinals and Reds didn't make any big moves either, even though the Cardinals had a gigantic hole at shortstop.

There had been rumblings that the Pirates' series of deadline moves the previous season had hurt their team chemistry. That dubious explanation helped Huntington avoid too much criticism for failing to upgrade in 2013. Also, the Pirates faithful was too busy feeling good to worry about it much. The Bucs had the best record in baseball, and their fans took pleasure in arguing that baseball's best team didn't *need* to upgrade. That didn't make much sense, but it felt great to say.

As the Pirates continued winning, the community at Bucs Dugout became less analytical than in years past. On nights when the Bucs won, it became common for the first 30-plus comments of a game recap to consist largely of celebrating. Commenters counted down the number of wins remaining until the Pirates hit 82 by posting pictures of players who wore those numbers. When the Bucs won their 65th game and had 17 wins left to reach 82, readers posted pictures of Bob Walk and Drew Sutton wearing No. 17. With 15 wins left, it was Manny Mota, Denny Neagle and Doug Drabek.

As the number of wins remaining dropped below 20, commenters also posted team photos of teams from the losing streak – for 15 wins remaining, it was the 2007 Pirates, who were the Bucs' 15th straight losing team. Clearly, there wasn't anything wonderful about those teams, and it seemed odd to see celebratory pictures of now-irrelevant players like Andy LaRoche and Jose Castillo. Usually when a Pirates fan mentions disappointing past players, it's ironic, or it's part of a cautionary tale. But the pictures that appeared on Bucs Dugout were neither. In fact, they were loving, almost – a fan's way of saying, "I forgive you." The Pirates were finally winning, and its fans were putting the losing streak to rest.

More than that, there just wasn't much to disagree about. Discussions at Bucs Dugout were sprinkled liberally with humorous pictures and GIFs. Pirates fans began acting like fans of other teams, who don't problematize every win.

Meanwhile, the Pirates began to attract notice from outside Pittsburgh. OVAthletics' Travis Berardi noted that, by early August, national writers like Tom Verducci and Tim Kurkjian and former MLB stars like Cal Ripken and John Smoltz had made appearances at PNC. NBC Sports' Craig Calcaterra noticed Pirates fans "coming out of the woodwork" in Columbus, three hours west of Pittsburgh. "I wore my Pirates cap out in public last night and people got excited," he wrote. "I think Pirates fans are starting to accept that this team is not going to crater on them and leave them sad for the [21st] year in a row." Calcaterra noted that the Pirates had become a "fashionable rooting interest" among baseball fans who didn't follow a particular team.

Still, at least in some quarters, every loss induced fears that the team would fall apart as it had in 2011 and 2012. Well into the second half, fans veered violently from mood to mood, and "collapse" was the key word on their lips. After two losses to the Rockies at Coors Field in early August, one fan wrote, "[The] '12 collapse began in [an] eerily similar way: uncharacteristic losses August 9-10 to NL West teams," referring to two losses to the Padres on those dates in 2012. "Jesus, losing [a] series to THE ROCKIES!!! Those are the type of things that start a collapse!" wrote another.

"I can't help it – I feel the same way, too," Wilbur Miller told me in August. "Logically, I look at it … I can't imagine a complete collapse happening." But it was hard to shake the feeling that a collapse was coming. "The fear is still there after the last two years. I think any normal person would have trouble putting that out of their mind."

Predictions of a collapse were simply defense mechanisms, Miller says. "You come to expect it, and so you're not disappointed."

"This season has been a delight and I've been genuinely excited for every game this year," wrote one Bucs Dugout reader. "I was hoping everyone would feel the same way, but I think the Pirates having the best record in baseball at points has spoiled the fan base, and the collapses from the past two years have put everyone on the brink."

That may have been overstating it, but it was true that the predictions of a collapse after every loss were exhausting. In August, the fretting reached a fever pitch when Starling Marte dropped a routine fly ball in the ninth inning that turned into a game-tying run by the Cardinals. The Pirates went on to lose, 4-3, in 14 innings. Around that time, an @BestFansPirates Twitter account sprang up, collecting Bucs fans' hysterical reactions to whatever the Pirates had failed to do perfectly that day. Fans predicted the team's season was effectively over and argued that Marte's drop had triggered "Collapse 3.0."

By themselves, a couple hundred agitated tweets don't prove much. For most fan bases, overheated, irrational reactions are a key part of the experience. But Pirates fans' reactions to their team's losses became increasingly aggressive.

Still, it wasn't hard to see where these fans were coming from. It's difficult to take a team seriously and then not feel hurt when it fails to come through. And for the third year running, the Pirates had played much better than expected for the first two-thirds of the season. After the collapses of the two previous seasons, what were fans *supposed* to think would happen?

"The results from the past two seasons do not influence my expectations for the last two months of this year's season. Not at all," a Bucs Dugout commenter wrote. "Nevertheless, the scars from the last two years are still pretty fresh, and ... I'm not going to take it for granted that either the countdown to a winning record or to a playoff spot will get to zero."

Nonetheless, weeks passed, and the collapse simply didn't materialize. As August turned to September, the Bucs didn't maintain their 100-win-type pace, but they got big victories when they needed them, taking two of three against San Diego and two of four in San Francisco in mid-August. They lost two of three to Milwaukee, but made up for that by taking two of three from the Cardinals, who they were battling for first place.

The Pirates also helped themselves with a pair of late-August deals. Trades in August are more complex than trades in July, since teams must subject big-league players to waivers before they can be traded – either a player gets claimed, in which case he can only be traded to the team doing the claiming, or he passes through waivers, in which case he can be traded anywhere.

The Bucs got lucky that outfielder Marlon Byrd of the Mets, who was in the midst of an unexpected career year at age 36 and whose salary was a mere $700,000, was still around for them to claim. The Reds, for example, had waiver priority on the Pirates, were in the midst of a playoff race against them, and could have used Byrd themselves, and yet they let him slip through to the Pirates. Neal Huntington claimed both Byrd and Mets catcher John Buck, and worked out a deal to get them both in exchange for reliever Vic Black and prospect Dilson Herrera. Buck replaced Tony Sanchez as the backup to Russell Martin, and Byrd immediately upgraded the Pirates' outfield.

The Pirates also swung a more minor trade for Twins first baseman Justin Morneau, giving up outfielder Alex Presley and reliever Duke Welker. Unlike Byrd, Morneau was well past his peak. But he could still hit righties, and Garrett Jones was struggling while playing first base against right-handed pitching. The Morneau trade was greeted oddly by fans and by the media, some of whom suggested it meant the Pirates were "all-in" in a way that they hadn't been in years past – as if, for example, Wandy Rodriguez, who they acquired near the July deadline in 2012, hadn't been a much better player than Morneau. But the Byrd trade was a big one, and Byrd made his presence felt immediately with a three-run homer in his first game with the Bucs.

By September 2, the Pirates were a game up on the Cards after having won their 80th game of the season. Their losing streak was about to bite the dust, and with about a month left to play.

I remember being unsure how I'd feel. After the Pirates won No. 80, I thought about how they had the chance to clinch a non-losing season in their next game, and it didn't really do much for me. But their 81st win, which occurred the next day, turned out to be a cathartic moment, the first of many. Byrd broke a 2-2 tie with an eighth-inning double off Brandon Kintzler, but the Brewers tied the game again in the bottom of the inning on Jean Segura's RBI single. Leading off the top of the ninth, Travis Snider worked a 2-2 count against Jim Henderson, then golfed a slider to right-center on the seventh pitch of the at-bat. That gave Bucs a 4-3 lead, and they finished the Brewers off as Khris Davis whiffed on Mark Melancon's breaking ball in the dirt.

The game was in Milwaukee, but in Pittsburgh and among Pirates fans throughout the country, the win inspired a ton of celebratory high-fives, both real and virtual. "I'm sleeping in my Pirates gear tonight like a little kid," wrote a Bucs Dugout commenter.

Others reflected on where they were when the streak began. "I was 26," wrote one. "That was two marriages, four cats, three dogs, innumerable fish, 50 pounds (added) and a whole head of black hair (now gray) ago."

The Bucs dropped the finale in Milwaukee, then got swept in a series at St. Louis in which a win or two would have dramatically improved their chances of winning the division. All four losses were by four runs or more, as the Bucs' offense foundered against Adam Wainwright and then rookie Michael Wacha in the last two losses.

Some part of me wondered about the possibility that the Pirates would lose their last 20 games in a row and end the season at 81-81 – that seemed like a perfectly Pirate-y ending. That possibility was far too remote to fret *too* much about, but the Bucs' awful four-game run did have me worried in a way I hadn't been before, particularly because all four starting pitchers involved (Francisco Liriano, A.J. Burnett, Jeff Locke and Charlie Morton) had struggled.

The Pirates' first winning season in 21 years arrived unexpectedly. Immediately after the Cardinals series, the Pirates were in Texas, facing one of baseball's best pitchers in Yu Darvish, who had struck out ten or more batters in five of his previous eight starts. But Gerrit Cole, who had turned 23 the day before, looked like a seasoned pro against the Rangers, pitching with purpose and racking up nine strikeouts over seven innings. Darvish was as good as advertised, but with two outs in the seventh, Byrd doubled to left, and Pedro Alvarez followed him with a double into the gap.

That made it 1-0 Pirates, and it would stay that way. Melancon came on in the ninth and got two groundouts before allowing a single. He then got A.J. Pierzynski to ground out harmlessly to second, and as the ball reached Gaby Sanchez's glove, Andrew McCutchen began walking in from the outfield, raising his arms and looking toward the heavens. It wasn't, "We did it." It was, "Thank goodness *that's* over." And so Cole, who had also pitched in win No. 81 (although he wasn't credited with the victory), ended up leading the Pirates to win No. 82 as well. Finally, the streak was history.

After the game, the Pirates said it wasn't a crucial milestone for them. After all, *they* hadn't been around for the entire 20-year losing streak. A few, like Cole, were in diapers when it started. "I've never suffered through anything for 20 years. I don't think there's anybody in here who has," Cole told the media. "I don't know if there's anybody that doesn't live in Pittsburgh that fully understands it."

That was an admirably modest stance, and perhaps an accurate one. In a way, it's a shame that the player most responsible for the win that broke the streak was a 23-year-old rookie from Southern California. He didn't understand what he'd done, and it was possible he never would, having not played for the Pirates when they were bad. But even the player best equipped to appreciate the end of the streak, Pittsburgh native Neil Walker, downplayed its significance.

"It's probably more important to me than anybody in this room, but – I don't mean to beat a dead horse – it's just a stepping stone in the direction we're trying to go as a team and as an organization," Walker told reporters.

The players might have had their sights set higher than a winning season, but many fans seemed so happy they could scarcely articulate a coherent thought. Many of the comments in the Bucs Dugout recap that night were variations on "WHOOOOOOO" and "YEAAAAAAHHHH," or celebratory pictures and GIFs.

"Regardless of what happens in the next two months, the 2013 Pittsburgh Pirates will forever be my favorite team," went one comment. "Not a single person on this team should ever have to buy a beer in the city of Pittsburgh again."

The Pirates kept going, taking the next two games to sweep the Rangers and increase their win total to 84. Then they came home to Pittsburgh, where fans greeted them with a long, cathartic standing ovation. The fans then watched Jeff Locke and the Pirates defeat the Cubs, moving back into a tie for first in the NL Central. The Pirates then dropped a 5-4 game in which Jason Grilli, then returning from injury, gave up a two-run homer in the seventh, but won the last two games of the series, after which they were a remarkable 87-62.

And then came the Padres. San Diego entered the series 28-10 all-time at PNC Park. That didn't mean anything, of course, particularly given the quality of the Pirates teams the Padres had played to accumulate that record. Too much is made of statistics like these, as the Pirates showed in 2013 when they outplayed the Brewers at Miller Park, where the Brew Crew had previously dominated them. But as the Padres coasted to victories in each of the first two games of the series, it was hard not to think about the Pirates' struggles against them at PNC.

In the first matchup, Andrew Cashner, a big righty with an explosive fastball, took a perfect game into the seventh inning. The Pirates stung some line drives that the Padres caught, and they eventually did get a hit from Jose Tabata in the seventh. But it was an ugly game overall.

The offense continued to look listless in a 5-2 loss against Eric Stults the following day. Worse, the Pirates had to suffer through a terrific performance from former shortstop Ronny Cedeno, who went 3-for-4 and made a couple of nice throws. Then the Pirates lost another, with Mark Melancon uncharacteristically blowing a save.

The Bucs continued to struggle in a crucial series against the Reds, who were bearing down on them for the top Wild Card spot. Melancon blew another save in the series opener as Jordy Mercer and Pedro Alvarez struggled to field ground balls. A.J. Burnett led the Pirates to a win in the second game with a 12-strikeout performance, but Jeff Locke gave up five runs in the first inning the following day as the Pirates fell 11-3.

After that day, the Pirates stood two games behind the Cardinals in the NL Central, and they were tied with the Reds for the top Wild Card spot. Given how well the Pirates had played in the first half of the season, their play down the stretch was less inspiring.

Dry Land

But the season was nearly over, and they were still squarely in line for a playoff berth.

Nonetheless, Pirates fans panicked over their team's play, particularly the series opener against the Reds. Joe Starkey of the *Tribune-Review* penned a "survival guide" for Bucs fans not used to dealing with the pressure of a playoff race. "If you can't handle it, get out now," he wrote. "There is often no rhyme or reason to what happens."

It was good advice. Pirates fans' panicking stemmed from the fact that they simply weren't used to following a playoff team over a 162-game season, in which even great teams will lose a couple times a week. And while the Pirates never really did collapse, it was easy to see why a fan base that had watched consecutive collapses would worry about the possibility that a third was on the way. The Bucs weren't exactly running the table late in the year, going 14-14 in August and 10-11 in September heading into their last two series of the season.

Still, the Pirates had held on long enough. They headed to Chicago with an 89-67 record and a chance to clinch a playoff berth, and they took a quick lead in the series opener when Neil Walker hit an opposite-field homer. Charlie Morton pitched seven scoreless innings, and the Pirates held a 1-0 lead until the eighth, when Donnie Murphy tied the game with an RBI single. But Starling Marte gave the Pirates a 2-1 lead with a towering home run in the ninth, pumping his fists as the ball flew over Wrigley Field's left-field wall.

The Pirates would only need to hang on in the bottom of the ninth, and they almost didn't. The Cubs had Nate Schierholtz on first in the bottom of the inning when Marlon Byrd misplayed a flare by Ryan Sweeney. Schierholtz came charging around the bases as McCutchen picked up the ball and chucked it toward the infield. The ball ended up near the mound, and it briefly looked like no one would be there to field it. But Justin Morneau lumbered across the infield just in time and threw home, where Schierholtz barreled into Russell Martin. Martin flipped over and held the ball straight up in triumph. Jason Grilli, who had been backing Martin up at the plate, bent to hug him. After 21 years, the Pirates were headed back to the playoffs.

The Bucs took two of three against their Cubs, then swept the Reds to complete the regular season. The Pirates hadn't kept pace with the Cardinals, who ultimately clinched the NL Central. But the Bucs did finish with 94 regular-season wins and clinched home-field advantage in a one-game playoff, also against Cincinnati.

It didn't seem right that the Pirates had clinched the top Wild Card spot after 20 straight losing seasons, and yet had to play one game for their postseason lives. I feared a scenario where the Pirates would lose the one-game playoff, then go back to their losing ways the following season. That seemed unlikely, but then so much of what the Pirates had done over the course of the streak had seemed unlikely.

It would be a tough matchup. Reds starter Johnny Cueto had tortured weaker Pirates teams for years, and the Reds' lineup was formidable. To counter that lineup, the Pirates picked lefty Francisco Liriano, whose brilliant slider would be tough for the Reds' best hitters – Joey Votto, Shin-Soo Choo and Jay Bruce, all left-handers – to deal with.

In any case, the city of Pittsburgh was pumped. The day before their home matchup against the Reds, Frank Coonelly and Clint Hurdle spoke at a large rally in Market Square. An enormous rubber duck started showing up in the Allegheny River. (The duck, a project created by Dutch artist Florentijn Hofman, wasn't made with the Pirates in mind, but given its arrival in the water behind PNC Park's right-field wall right before the playoffs began, it sure *felt* like it was.) And injured catcher Michael McKenry suggested that Pirates fans wear all black to the Bucs' home playoff game, an idea that the fans eagerly spread.

It worked. 40,000 Pirates fans arrived at the game overwhelmingly dressed in black, and PNC Park sounded like a European

Dry Land

soccer stadium. It was absurdly loud from the pre-game introductions through the first several innings.

In the second inning, Cueto left a changeup high in the zone for Marlon Byrd, who smashed it to left to give the Pirates a 1-0 lead. Pirates fans began to taunt the Reds starter, shouting "Cue-to! Cue-to!" in unison, much as Red Sox fans had shouted "Dar-ryl!" at the Mets' Darryl Strawberry in the 1986 World Series. The fans' ridiculously loud chanting seemed to rattle Cueto (although he denied it after the game), and, with Russell Martin at the plate, Cueto dropped the ball before getting set to deliver. The fans let him have it. "This standing-room-only crowd is trying to get under Johnny Cueto's skin, and they might be," TBS announcer Ernie Johnson said as it happened.

On the next pitch, just seconds later, Cueto threw a fastball right down the middle, and Martin delivered a shot to left-center to make it 2-0 Pirates. It was Martin's home run, of course, but the fans deserved a share of the credit. Throughout most of his career, Cueto had owned the Pirates, but on this night, Pirates fans owned *him*.

On the other side of the ball, the Reds had no answer for Francisco Liriano. He completely neutralized Votto, and there were several plate appearances against Reds lefties where Liriano threw nothing but sliders. The Reds' lineup didn't contain much in the way of serious threats against left-handed pitching. Amusingly, the right-handed Byrd would have provided one – the Reds had inexplicably failed to block the Pirates from claiming Byrd, and now not only was he beating them, but the Reds were also failing against a left-handed pitcher who Byrd might have been able to hit.

The Pirates added another run in the third on Pedro Alvarez's sacrifice fly, then drove Cueto out of the game when Starling Marte doubled in the fourth. Neil Walker followed with a double of his own off reliever Sean Marshall. After intentionally walking Andrew McCutchen and walking Justin Morneau, Marshall got Byrd to hit into a tailor-made double play, but Brandon Phillips flubbed it, and Walker came home. The Pirates got another run in the seventh on

Martin's second homer of the game, a solo shot off Logan Ondrusek.

After the third inning, there was never much doubt about the outcome, and when it was over, the Pirates had won, 6-2, and they were headed to the NLDS to take on the Cardinals. Meanwhile, the Reds, frustrated by their team's performance against the Pirates in the one-game playoff and in the series that ended the regular season, fired manager Dusty Baker days later.

And so the Bucs headed to St. Louis, and it was hard not to feel like they had momentum on their side. Baseball doesn't care about how things feel, though, and Game 1 of the NLDS went poorly. A.J. Burnett's curveball wasn't working, and the Cards pelted him for seven runs. Several of those came after a hit by pitch and two straight walks, which should have been more information than Clint Hurdle needed that Burnett's night was over. Meanwhile, Adam Wainwright limited the Pirates to three hits over seven innings.

The Pirates made up for that stinker of a night with a brilliant performance in Game 2, however. Gerrit Cole, who was seemingly improving as the year progressed, pitched six terrific innings, with Yadier Molina's fifth-inning solo home run as his only blemish.

Pedro Alvarez led a Pirates offense that surged for seven runs. Alvarez hit a one-out ground-rule double in the second, then came home when Cole, the Pirates' best-hitting pitcher, grounded a single up the middle. The next inning, Morneau singled, and Alvarez hit a bomb to center field. Then Mercer doubled in the fifth, and Byrd followed with a ground-rule double of his own. As Byrd's hit bounced over the wall, Cardinals starter Lance Lynn held his hand to his face, looking like a five-year-old who had accidentally dropped his favorite toy down the stairs. The Pirates added another run in the sixth, and then a Starling Marte solo homer in the eighth. They coasted to an easy 7-1 win, returning to Pittsburgh with the series tied at one.

Fans greeted the Pirates with another packed house for Game 3, and the Bucs got on the board first. Andrew McCutchen reached in the first inning via a walk, and Justin Morneau then hit a ground-er up the middle that bounced off pitcher Joe Kelly. Cardinals shortstop Pete Kozma got to the ball late and made a poor throw to first, and the Bucs wound up with runners at second and third. Byrd then punched them in with a single past David Freese. Carlos Beltran tied the score with a two-run single in the fifth, and the two teams traded punches in the late innings, but the Bucs finally pulled away, scoring two runs off Carlos Martinez in the eighth. The Pi-rates thus needed to win just one of two games to eliminate the Cardinals and move on to the NLCS.

Unfortunately, they would have to face St. Louis' nearly unhit-table rookie Michael Wacha in Game 4. The Pirates had come up empty in seven innings against Wacha's toxic fastball/changeup combination in a regular-season game a month before, and Wacha had struck out 23 batters in three starts since then. The Cardinals had also driven Pirates starter Charlie Morton crazy during the reg-ular season, knocking one seeing-eye single after another en route to a .937 OPS in three starts against him.

As it turned out, Morton held his own against Wacha, trading zeroes through the first five innings. In the sixth, though, he walked leadoff batter Beltran, then gave up a deep fly ball to Matt Holliday. McCutchen climbed the fence in pursuit, then held on to the top of the wall for several seconds as it flew 20 feet over his head. It was a deflating moment – a two-run lead against Wacha and the Cardi-nals' flame-throwing bullpen felt like a big one indeed. The Pirates did get one run back on an Alvarez solo homer in the eighth, but they never seriously threatened to tie the game as Martinez and Trevor Rosenthal closed the door.

That set up a Game 5 matchup on October 9. It was my birthday. I don't like attention on birthdays, and I usually spend them alone. I happened to be working my last day at a part-time job at a small music school. I'd only been there five months before quitting, but the end of that job still triggered a bit of nostalgia. While I was working that day, I found out about a shooting in my hometown of

Wheeling, in which the father of a former classmate of mine fired dozens of shots into a government building my father had played a role in creating years before. No one died but the shooter, but I called my dad to make sure he hadn't been there. It turned out he hadn't, and that very few people had, due to the government shutdown that was happening at the time. I arrived home shortly after the game began, already in a strange mood.

23-year-old Gerrit Cole (starting, after some controversy, in place of A.J. Burnett) handled himself well, striking out five over five innings. But in the second, after giving up a two-out walk to Jon Jay, Cole missed his spot on a slider to David Freese, who hit a line drive that just cleared the wall in left.

Meanwhile, the Pirates couldn't make anything happen against Adam Wainwright, despite Wainwright's uncharacteristically shaky command. Wainwright struck out six and allowed eight hits, but benefited from the Bucs lining into two unlikely double plays.

With the Pirates down 2-0 and a man on in the top of the sixth, Clint Hurdle sent Garrett Jones to pinch-hit for Cole, obviously a sensible decision, but one that resulted in the Pirates completely blowing their chances to win. Jones flied out and Starling Marte hit into a double play, and then Justin Wilson entered and gave up an insurance run to make it 3-0. The Pirates picked up a run in a bizarre seventh inning that featured three infield singles, but in the eighth, Mark Melancon allowed a single to Matt Holliday, then a two-run homer to Matt Adams. Pete Kozma singled in a run later in the inning, but by then the Pirates' likelihood of victory was already close to zero. Justin Morneau and Marlon Byrd singled in the ninth, but Wainwright whiffed Alvarez to end the Pirates' season.

It had been an underwhelming series – Alvarez and Byrd had accounted for almost all of the Pirates' offense, and Marte and Neil Walker had combined to go 1-for-38. But it was nothing to be ashamed of. Cole, Francisco Liriano, Charlie Morton, and most of the Pirates' relievers had held their own, with Burnett and Melancon as the only pitchers who had really struggled. (Pity poor Melancon, who gave up two homers in the NLDS after allowing just one the entire regular season.) The Pirates had gotten their full playoff series, including two loud, thrilling games at PNC Park.

I was disappointed that the Pirates hadn't advanced, but mostly I felt grateful that I had witnessed an incredible season, and finally seen the end of an era. The birthday, the job, the shooting and the end of the season pressed themselves upon me, and I teared up, happy to be alive. It had been 21 years since 1992. Thousands upon thousands of Pirates fans who had lived through the glory days of the 1960s and 1970s hadn't made it all the way through the streak, and I felt grateful to have been there for the beginning and to have lived to see the end. I thought of older Pirates fans, people who had been in their thirties or forties in 1979, when the Bucs last won the World Series. Those folks were now in their sixties or seventies or eighties, and I felt happy that they were still here. And I also felt glad for Pirates fans in their teens or early twenties who were now watching a winning Pirates team for the first time. Baseball is, ultimately, a trivial thing, but it provides a background for more important events in our lives, and after more than two decades, that background had finally changed.

I wrote something similar at Bucs Dugout, which may have affected the responses in the comments, but the overwhelming response to the end of the Pirates' season was gratitude.

"As much as no one wants it to be over, this is still the best season we've had in decades," wrote one fan. "It will always be remembered, and we will never feel quite like we all did this year."

A number of fans predicted that the Pirates' strong 2013 season was just the beginning, and it was hard to disagree with them. With a solid core of major-league talent (led, of course, by Andrew McCutchen, who won the NL MVP award), a good minor-league system, a credible plan for winning at the big-league level (Clint Hurdle earned his 2013 NL Manager of the Year honors with a terrific shift-heavy defensive strategy) and few worrisome payroll obligations, the Pirates could well have a streak of winning seasons ahead.

We simply don't know, however. A Kansas City Royals scenario, in which the Pirates end their losing streak with a winning season, only to begin another losing streak, isn't impossible. And while much of the Pirates' improvement in 2013 was legitimate, they *did* lean fairly heavily on veteran acquisitions like A.J. Burnett and Russell Martin. In any case, now, as I write this immediately after the season, seems like the wrong time for Bucs fans to worry much about the future. The losing streak is over, and for all anyone knows, the Pirates are in the midst of a streak of *winning* seasons that began in 2013.

Chapter 11

I'll probably just use the first name.

Eli, Eli.

How old are you?

I am 26.

And you're from?

I'm from Indiana, Pennsylvania.

So do you remember the '90 to '92 teams?

I was just talking to Doug, my cousin, about that. He's my cousin.

Yeah, he looked kind of like you.

I was five years old in '92. I think we remember it just because I was so into it as a kid. I collected baseball cards from when I was, like, two, and my aunt would go to a lot of games and get the programs and stuff, so I would learn about the team that way, maybe a few years later. I didn't know that they were one win, or one out,

Dry Land

from the World Series. But I knew they were good. I don't remember that much other than that. My family had moved from Bloomfield to Washington, Pennsylvania. We had just moved there. I was still five; my sister would have been ... three? And it was just all of us – her, me, my mom and my dad – on this pullout couch. We had just moved to this new house in Washington, Pennsylvania, in October of '92. So we'd watch the games on that and fall asleep.

So you were maybe too young to really process what you were seeing.

Yes. It wasn't until a few years later when I realized exactly what had happened.

Did you stick with the Pirates through all their losing?

Yeah. I've always just been a big baseball fan, so I guess that's helped me to kind of stick with this, because even if I didn't like the Pirates, I would just be watching baseball in general.

I got really sick of it towards the end of the Littlefield era. I always felt good about Huntington. I always thought they were doing a good job. I could see what they were trying to do. So once that happened, I didn't have any reservations about giving the team money, or whatever. But even through probably about '05 or so, I realized, I'm still a fan now, I'll always be a fan. If this doesn't turn me away, I might as well stick through it, because they're bound to win at some point if [I] do. [It will] feel better when they finally do it, having gone through that.

And last year it was. It just added to it so much last October [and] the whole season. I just remember trying to meet people who were going to the Wild Card game, just people I knew, I wanted to meet them and shake their hand before the game. My one friend, we were just talking – we remember scalping tickets for five dollars to see them play in 2006 or something, to see some terrible display of baseball. Now we're here at a playoff game together.

Like, "We've been through hell together."

Exactly.

So 2006 would be the depths of the despair, and you would [have been about] 19 then?

Um, yeah.

But you still thought they would come out of it at some point?

In '05 or '06, I figured eventually. I remember tricking myself into being excited about Jeromy Burnitz or something. Looking back, that's how I had to get through that.

I do remember, toward the end of Littlefield's tenure, having no faith in him and no faith in the team in general, but just being like, "They're my team."

When did you know the Neal Huntington era would be different?

The '08 draft, just taking [Pedro] Alvarez. That was different. And I know just doing what you're supposed to do didn't necessarily mean that they were anything special. But I just liked the moves they would make. Even the trades that didn't necessarily work out, they weren't worried about patches for the time being. They weren't worried about winning 75 games just to save some face.

How many games did you go to this year?

Probably about 50 or 60.

Looking back on the season now, how has it changed your perspective as a fan?

Dry Land

Part of it is the weight coming off the shoulders as far as them finally [having] a winning season. I always hated when people would get so mad, as if [the Pirates] were supposed to go sign one free agent and try and improve upon a 75-win team, as if that would make much of a difference. I understood the frustration behind that, but people [would] say that year after year, as if going over .500 is some sort of a goal, or you get some medal for it. The fact that [a winning season] happened, at least, lifts a weight, and you don't have to hear that all the time anymore. You're no longer second-class citizens.

I like the Steelers and Penguins, but not like I love the Pirates. In a way, that kept me being a fan sometimes, that a lot of people didn't care or would almost rip you for being a Pirates fan, when they support the other two teams. The fact that they're up there with [the Steelers and Penguins], and seeing other people want to join in on that, in a way, it was neat.

The fact that I was able to go to a playoff game – a *Pirates* playoff game – things like that that I would daydream about. As much as I figured that they'll have to eventually do something, just by probability, [in] my lifetime, there's always a fear of, "Is that *ever* going to happen? 20, 30 years from now, are we going to be still waiting for that?" Just the fact that that happened and I got to have that experience.

I feel almost like a fan of the other teams. You get to talk about playoffs every once in a while, and you get to go into a season next year, whether they do anything or not, at least with some expectation of some success. It's what everyone else does, but it's a novelty, in a way.

We can approach this offseason like, "These players need to be able to contribute to a playoff-caliber team," rather than just being like, "This guy'll fill some space for a couple years."

Yeah.

Charlie Wilmoth

20 years is a long time. For 20 years, we so rarely had the opportunity to think of anything as having any meaning.

Yeah, and we watch everything from a different perspective than other teams. There are other teams I like better than others, but they're still *other teams*. It was never *my team*. It was never the Pirates in the playoffs or in contention. [Even] 2011 was such a special year for me, just because, finally, after the age of five, I got to see games that were meaningful. I feel like it's something that, I'm still kind of going through the experience. Even this [offseason] is new to me. Next year, Opening Day, it'll still be new. I'm still in that mode where things are new.

Is this an emotional thing for you?

Yeah. To me, it was just something, having gone through that … I remember the moment I realized they traded Aramis Ramirez, just being crushed. And then just sticking through that, like I said, going to games in '05 and '06 with friends that I would go to games with this year. You know, we were here for that, and that makes this so much better. And it's hard for me to articulate what it means emotionally, just because they were always my favorite team. Of all sports.

Maybe there's something that I connected with the Pirates more just because everyone wanted to trash them for so long. Whatever makes people not just turn away from the team, or not invest so much emotionally, at least, for whatever reason, I just never stopped doing that. I guess I'm glad that happened.

You're glad that the streak happened?

No. I'm glad that I stuck through it. I never got sucked into, you know, "Baseball sucks. The Pirates suck." A lot of people my age had that apathy. Going through school, the Steelers, or the NFL, you could just talk about with anybody. Baseball, there were only a select few people that could even carry on a conversation. I imagine it [was] very different growing up in Western Pennsylvania when I did than [it was] for a lot of Pirates fans before. It would have been neat to have grown up when they were relevant, and have memories of the seventies, or something like that. I'm not happy the streak happened, but it is what it is. A year ago, maybe I wouldn't say that. It's just part of the Pirates' history and part of my life of being a fan. It shaped me in ways that I probably don't even realize.

It's been a big part of our lives.

Exactly, yeah. Just knowing the people that stuck with it too, it's almost like a special kind of a bond. I don't get on Facebook that much, but I [posted] a status update, just mentioned all these people I knew [over] the years. I think it was after the 82nd win, just thanking people for being along for the ride with me. Just being able to share that with people. I don't necessarily have a problem with people jumping on the bandwagon. I have a problem with people that were …

Trashing them before?

People who were trashing them, or wondering why you're a fan of the team. We still always have a tailgate – Opening Day, and then the last home game. We're just there. Obviously, in September, there's a lot less interest. This was maybe 2010 or '11. And some guy just happens to be walking down the street. The Steelers weren't playing that day, but he was wearing some Steelers shirt. He's like, "What are you guys doing?" We're like, "We're tailgating for the baseball game." He's like, "I could see you doing that for a football game, but I don't understand why you're doing that here." And that stuck with me. There were a couple people that were upset by the guy. People like that … if you don't like it, whatever, but he's, like, angry that we're fans.

But if people weren't baseball fans and this makes them baseball fans, good. Kids – good for them. They don't know how lucky they are to be kids now. That, or people who don't watch sports as much, if they get excited about the Pirates, good. I'm glad they could be drawn in.

One other thing that you might be interested in … a lot of times, I would keep a scorecard. I got to know some of the early '90s teams from my aunt, who would go to a lot of games. She would give me all the programs, and I would look at scoresheets and piece together the games. I found one that was a '91 NLCS program. It was only filled in – it stopped scoring for the last few innings. I've had it for a long time. I went and looked it up, and it was the other Game 7. I found that the day of, or the day before, the [2013] Wild Card game. It was like, "I get to fill out my own playoff scorecard." Things like that mean a lot to me. These things that I've sort of envied or hoped for finally happened.

Conclusion

It's November 2013. The Pirates' division rivals in St. Louis went to the World Series. The weather is awful. Life goes on.

The Pirates' persistent losing was a part of the rhythm of life, not only from day to day, but from year to year, in about the same way the sun dictates not only the time of dawn and dusk but also the changing of the seasons.

During the school year, I teach music at a small liberal arts college. In the spring and fall, I lecture in the mornings and early afternoons, write music or grade for a couple hours, and squeeze in bits of blogging here and there before the game comes on in the evening. I often watch while folding laundry or cooking. Sometimes I watch with a book, turning the sound down during commercial breaks to read a couple pages. If I go out, I watch a compressed game when I get home. In the spring, baseball seems miraculous, and the possibilities for the Pirates seem endless. In the fall, it can be a slog, but thanks to the expansion of rosters to 40, there are always new players to watch, and plenty of reasons to tune in.

As spring becomes summer, the semester ends, and watching the game becomes life itself, as opposed to just a contrast with whatever I had been doing earlier that day. Some years, I'll take some sort of summer job in addition to writing about baseball, but I always have more time in the summer than I do during the school year. In Pittsburgh, the seats at PNC fill with sunbathers and revelers and schoolchildren. As my own focus sharpens, I can feel the city's sharpening too. Fan attendance usually peaks in June, and the first two summer months are huge for baseball geeks, with the draft at the beginning of June and the trade deadline at the end of July.

The waning of each Pirates' season is a reminder that, soon, the weather will turn cold, and we will turn our attention to boring things like leaf-raking and football. The changing of sports as the weather changes was probably a factor in my becoming a baseball fan in the first place. Baseball arrives as the trees begin to bloom. The appearance of televised baseball reminds us that the days are getting longer and that school will soon be out. The end of the baseball season means that the days will soon be dark by 5:30, and in the morning we'll be bundled up and trudging wearily off to class.

The Pirates add color to the tapestry of Pittsburgh. During the streak, they weren't a vital cultural force, which was sad. But we got through it. Each year, the ice melted, and we returned to our seats and our televisions. Parents bonded with their children. Young people pored over statistics. Couples went to PNC on dates. We did those things in smaller numbers than we would have if the Pirates had been winners, but we still did them. 20 years of losing didn't stop us. On some level, the losing was a burden and an annoyance. But on a deeper level, it was irrelevant. We kept coming back because of the way the Pirates fit into our lives.

Self-pity is unbecoming. In his book *The Whore of Akron*, Scott Raab describes his reaction to a playoff loss by his beloved Cleveland Cavaliers. Not even a season-ending loss – just a Game 4 loss to the Orlando Magic.

> I began to cry. Quietly, at first. Followed by soft moaning. Soft, I say: I really didn't want my wife to hear me. But she did, and she came downstairs.
> "What's *wrong*?"
> "They can't beat Orlando," I said. "It isn't going to happen."
> She came over to the chair and bent to hug me.

"I'm never going to see it," I sniffled. "Not even with LeBron."

"Oh, baby," she said, pressing my head to her belly.

"You think maybe I could get a handjob?"

My immediate reaction upon reading this – and pardon my French – was, "What a fucking baby."

Fan bases of losing teams are frequently characterized as "long-suffering." But one should only allow oneself to suffer so much. The psychological effects of rooting for a losing team are real, but the fan needs to compensate by compartmentalizing. The Pirates went 20 years between winning seasons. I did a lot in those 20 years. Most Pirates fans did. And when I'm old and I think back on those 20 years of my life, I won't think about the Pirates' performance. I'll think about my family, my friends, the places I lived, the goals I pursued.

It could be that I don't know any better, that the Pirates' consistently poor performances throughout my adult life insulated me from any expectation that they might actually win, and thus from any true feeling of trauma as a result of their failures. I also have the benefit of imagining – if only in the back of my head – that I will live long enough to see the Bucs' fortunes change completely. Maybe Major League Baseball will institute a salary cap. Maybe the Pirates will draft the next Barry Bonds and the next Albert Pujols in consecutive seasons. Heck, maybe the Pirates' current young core of Andrew McCutchen, Gerrit Cole, Starling Marte, Gregory Polanco and Jameson Taillon is good enough to win a World Series. Who knows?

A fan in his or her seventies or eighties, who remembers the Pirates' World Series championships in 1960 and 1971 and 1979, likely wouldn't perceive the situation the same way. The point, though, is that, as fans, we shouldn't let a team define more than a small part of who we are. Our interpersonal relationships and our personal goals should be more important. We can't allow a game – an entertainment in which we, the fans, are at best bit players – to make us miserable. Like Jimmy Dugan said, "There's no crying in baseball." And there shouldn't be any pity handjobs, either.

Baseball is, first and foremost, a game. Pirates fans frequently call for Bob Nutting to sell the Pirates to a crazed billionaire who would run the team as if it were a charity case, spending tens of millions, or perhaps hundreds of millions, of his or her own money to force the Pirates into contention. It's a beautiful dream, until one considers that there aren't really any major-league teams that are run that way, and that, if you've got $50 million a year burning a hole in your pocket, there are far better ways to spend it than on a baseball team. On cancer research, for example. Or on feeding the homeless. The failures of sports teams are fake problems, even though every fan, me included, sometimes feels otherwise.

I follow the Penguins, and WVU basketball, but the Pirates are the only team I've ever really cared about. In my writing, my impatience with them frequently boils over into exasperation. But at the end of the day, the Bucs have been good to me. I'm an introvert and I can't stand small talk. The Pirates help me talk to my dad. They help me navigate the craggy terrain of adult friendships. The bonds I've formed with other fans online have helped get me through times when other aspects of my life haven't gone well. The Bucs are good for Pittsburgh, and good for people like me. I'm glad they exist, and despite my many frustrations, I don't regret the time I've spent following them.

PirateFest 2013 has been crammed into two December days instead of the usual three, and many of the Pirates' brightest stars are missing. Andrew McCutchen isn't here for the first day, and neither, as far as I can tell, are Pedro Alvarez, Gerrit Cole, Russell Martin, Francisco Liriano or Mark Melancon. Neil Walker and Jason Grilli are here, but many of the players present are rookies or journeymen. I'm part of a group of bloggers that interviews new catcher Chris Stewart, who's just come from the Yankees in a trade. He asks us where he can find housing.

I amble into the season-ticket-holder portion of the event. Black-and-gold-decorated booths cover the convention-center floor, and about a mile of fans queue up for Grilli's autograph. There's a beanbag toss and a caricaturist. It's almost as if you're on the boardwalk at the beach, except everything is black and gold, and it's freezing outside.

I wander to the stage in the far corner, where Frank Coonelly, Neal Huntington and Clint Hurdle answer fans' questions, as they do each year. At first, the scene seems familiar – a fan argues vehemently with Coonelly about the Pirates' television contract, shouting and interrupting him.

A few minutes later, though, a fan from Manheim, Pennsylvania, an hour and a half from Philadelphia, tells the Pirates' brain trust that she can now wear her Pirates gear in Phillies country without fear of being mocked. Many in the crowd applaud.

Then a kid from Punxsutawney walks up to the mic and practically bows at Huntington's feet. "Neal, you're my idol," he says.

Another fan says he arrived in Pittsburgh from the Detroit area in 1988, when he was ten. He thanks the Pirates' management for assembling a team that reminded him of the Jim Leyland-led clubs that were beginning their heyday when he arrived. Then a young fan from Fox Chapel tells the Pirates they've given him something to be proud of. A handful of fans pose challenging questions, but overall, the tenor of the Q+A is clearly different than it was last year, and the fans seem overwhelmingly grateful for the season they've just experienced.

Once one knows what to look for, the difference in the atmosphere is palpable even when watching the crowd from afar. Last year, there were many fans just sitting around, as if they didn't care about all the bells and whistles and were just there waiting for the Pirates to prove something to them. This year, more fans walk from place to place as if PirateFest really has something to offer.

I'm having trouble finding fans who have anything negative to say this year. If they're out there, they're hiding well. If the fans I talk to ever had issues with the team, they don't seem eager to

Dry Land

revisit them. In both the Q+A sessions and in interviews, it feels like a sense of order has been restored. Fans are no longer eager to rip each other, or the Pirates' management or ownership. Pirates fandom during the streak was complicated, and fans rooted in a way that was conflicted. That no longer appears to be the case.

Some problems fans do have with the Pirates now, in late 2013, tend to be good ones for the team. "Last year, there was a point where we were saying we kind of missed it when they weren't doing as well, because when you [went] down to the stadium you could actually walk," says Mary, a season ticket holder in her forties.

Some fans can't wait to talk about their own connections to the team. Richard, a 49-year-old from Beechview who's here with his 17-year-old nephew Julian, tells me his dad was Roberto Clemente's best friend. I have no way of verifying that, but now, after the Pirates' winning season, is the first time I've had fans lead with stories like that, when I'm not even asking about them. (Later, a fan tells me his son used to play in the Pirates' minor-league system.)

I ask Richard if he has any opinion of the Pirates' management or ownership. "I don't worry about that," he says. "Life's too short. I'm drama-free."

Julian, a high-school student, is basking in the first winning Pirates season of his lifetime.

Before 2013, Julian says, the Pirates were a niche interest at his school. "There were a select few [fans], but not much," he says.

Students at his school used to mock the few Pirates fans there. "Oh yeah, 'The Buccos suck, they're never going to win, I don't know why you support them,'" he says. "They're starting to come along more now that we're winning."

Richard and Julian aren't the only family members who have bonded over the Pirates' winning season.

"It's just something nice to share with your parents," says Jordan, an 18-year-old who attends Burgettstown High School. "My mom and dad saw this stuff happen before, but I never saw it. To

188

see the city respond to the Wild Card game and the playoff games against the Cardinals, it was really nice to see."

Jason is a 32-year-old season-ticket holder from Bridgeport, West Virginia – and if you're wondering how that's possible, his family got season tickets in 2013 and frequently drove an hour and 40 minutes to Pittsburgh for three-day weekends during homestands. Jason introduces himself by having his three-year-old son tell me who his favorite Pirate is. (It's "Anduh Mucun.") Like many Pirates fans, Jason's usual autumn priorities completely changed when the Bucs went on their postseason run.

"As an avid sports fan, [I'm] spoiled by the Steelers. I got to see three AFC championship games. And all of a sudden, it's September 15 and the Steelers have played three games, and I forgot," Jason says.

"Outside of getting married and having two little boys, that Tuesday-night Wild Card game is in the top three right after that," says Jason, who says he's watched the game six times on DVR. "It was one of those events that I looked at my brother and my wife and said, 'Listen, I'm not drinking, because I want to remember this. I want to enjoy this entire night.'"

As PirateFest winds down, the darkness outside begins to make the fluorescent lighting in the convention center seem increasingly unreal, and I have to blink more than usual to adjust. Above, blue neon lights trace the curve of the roof. The vastness of the room becomes more palpable as more and more fans head home for the night. The memorabilia merchants are still doing good business, probably because people are buying items they hadn't wanted to carry around all day. Exhausted parents carry their even-more-exhausted young children.

The Pirates' management and players are done speaking. The performance is over. Most of the festival's booths are still open, but the place has the feel of a bar at last call. PirateFest will wrap up tomorrow, and that will be the last occasion fans will gather en masse for the Pirates until spring training games begin.

Dry Land

I walk outside. Earlier in the day, it had been snowing, but now it's too warm, and a thick layer of slush smothers Pittsburgh's streets. The clacking of hard rain competes with the sounds of festivalgoers climbing into their cars and driving home. I look across the Allegheny River at PNC Park, and the lights above the stadium glow in soft blue. I feel a strange sense of calm. I walk toward my car, giving PNC one last glance and reminding myself that I'll see it again in April.

Thanks

Wilbur Miller, Stephen Catanese, Pete Wilmoth, Sam Wilmoth, David Todd, and Pat Lackey for their invaluable advice; my family; David Manel, Vlad and John Fredland at Bucs Dugout; Tim Williams, Brian McElhinny, Kevin Creagh, James Santelli, Ed Giles, Tom Smith and the rest of the Pirates blogging crew; Tim Dierkes and the rest of my friends at MLBTR; SB Nation; Rob King; Chris Mueller, Colin Dunlap and everyone else at 93.7 The Fan; Honor Forte; Rob Neyer; Daniel Dudley; Eric Simons and Daniel Wann; Allison Davis for the encouragement; Ryan Carra for helping me get back into baseball in the first place; Eli Nellis; Neil Clancy for noticing things I hadn't; Sam Dingman; Scott McCauley; David Hill; Anna Bracewell; Greg Allison; Ryan Hizer; Anthony Fabbricatore; Anne Trinh; Danny Shapira; Dan Szymborski; Travis Berardi; Travis Sawchik; John Perrotto; Mark Stacy; Adam Bittner, Anson Whaley and Aaron Hawley; Andy Chomos and Steve Zielinski; cocktailsfor2; Dan Hart, Terry Rodgers, and everyone else with the Pirates; BaseballReference.com and FanGraphs.com for making a project like this exponentially easier. This project also would have been considerably tougher were it not for the free availability of old articles from the *Post-Gazette* and the *Tribune-Review*. (Please see the citations that follow.) Last but not least, thanks to Bucs Dugout's readers, who were incredibly helpful in answering my questions. You can find quotes I've attributed to them at BucsDugout.com.

Chapter 1

Baseball-Reference.com. "Jason Kendall." http://www.baseball-reference.com/players/k/kendaja01.shtml

Baseball-Reference.com. "Pittsburgh Pirates team history & encyclopedia." http://www.baseball-reference.com/teams/PIT/

Cook, Ron. "Chad Hermansen: Another at-bat." Pittsburgh *Post-Gazette*, 9 July 2000. http://old.post-gazette.com/sports_headlines/20000709hermansen3.asp

Cook, Ron. "McClatchy villain in Pirates' demise." Pittsburgh *Post-Gazette*, 20 September 2000. http://old.post-gazette.com/sports/columnists/20000920cook.asp

Dvorchak, Robert. "Pirates and Meares agree to settle grievance, cut ties." Pittsburgh *Post-Gazette*, 30 October 2002. http://old.post-gazette.com/pirates/20021030bucs1030p4.asp

Dvorchak, Robert. "Young: No home-field edge when Pirates at PNC Park." Pittsburgh *Post-Gazette*, 19 May 2003. http://old.post-gazette.com/pirates/20030519bucside0519p6.asp

"Felony sentences in state courts – Statistical tables." Bureau of Justice Statistics, December 2009. http://www.bjs.gov/content/pub/pdf/fssc06st.pdf

Finley, Bill. "Playoff hero starting over again – Cabrera aims for majors." New York *Daily News*, 26 August 1998. http://www.nydailynews.com/archives/sports/playoff-hero-starting-cabrera-aims-majors-article-1.817418

Madden, Mark. "Madden: Baker's son gives us a series moment." Pittsburgh *Post-Gazette*, 26 October 2002. http://old.post-gazette.com/sports/columnists/20021026madden1026p1.asp

McCollough, J. Brady. "Nutting looks at big picture with Pirates." Pittsburgh *Post-Gazette*, 29 September 2013. http://www.post-gazette.com/stories/sports/pirates/nutting-looks-at-the-big-picture-with-pirates-705380/

Meyer, Paul. "Pirates 'Freak Show' hit zenith with July no-hitter." Pittsburgh *Post-Gazette*, 10 July 2007. http://www.post-gazette.com/pirates/2007/07/10/Pirates-Freak-Show-hit-zenith-with-July-no-hitter/stories/200707100154

Meyer, Paul. "Pirates Q+A with Paul Meyer." Pittsburgh *Post-Gazette*, 16 October 2002. http://old.post-gazette.com/pirates/questions/20021016bucqa.asp

Pearlman, Jeff. "Wistful thinking." *Sports Illustrated*, 31 August 1998. http://si.com/vault/article/magazine/MAG1013899/index.htm

Dry Land

"Plus: Baseball; Pirates sign Kendall to 6-year contract." The *New York Times*, 18 November 2000. http://www.nytimes.com/2000/11/18/sports/plus-baseball-pirates-sign-kendall-to-6-year-contract.html

Wojciechowski, Gene. "Pirates buried? Owner treasures them." Chicago *Tribune*, 24 March 1996. http://articles.chicagotribune.com/1996-03-24/sports/9603240167_1_pittsburgh-pirates-charlie-hayes-pirates-coaching-staff

Chapter 2

Biertempfel, Rob. "Biertempfel: Visit to Los Angeles in 2007 proved unheavenly for Bucs." Pittsburgh *Tribune-Review*, 22 June 2013. http://triblive.com/sports/pirates/4212502-74/pirates-2007-six#axzz2ekNIEjkJ

Callis, Jim. "Pirates tab Santiago as Kendall's successor." *Baseball America*, 16 December 2004. https://www.baseballamerica.com/news/041216santiago/

Cook, Ron. "Next in line? Bonifay aware that he could be fired if the losing continues." Pittsburgh *Post-Gazette*, 29 October 2000. http://old.post-gazette.com/sports/columnists/20001029cook.asp

Dvorchak, Robert. "Bonifay likes what he sees in team." Pittsburgh *Post-Gazette*, 3 April 2001, C4.

"The Italian job: Simon won't be charged in sausage race prank." The Associated Press, 10 July 2003. http://sportsillustrated.cnn.com/baseball/news/2003/07/09/sausage_assault_ap/

Kovacevic, Dejan. "Actor Keaton criticizes Pirates' owners before first pitch." Pittsburgh *Post-Gazette*, 10 April 2006. http://www.post-gazette.com/stories/local/breaking/actor-keaton-criticizes-pirates-owners-before-first-pitch-429451/

Kovacevic, Dejan. "Inside the Pirates: History for all eternity?" Pittsburgh *Post-Gazette*, 26 May 2007. http://www.post-gazette.com/stories/sports/pirates/inside-the-pirates-history-for-all-eternity-486792/

Kovacevic, Dejan. "Inside the Pirates: The MVP that got away." Pittsburgh *Post-Gazette*, 18 August 2007. http://www.post-gazette.com/stories/sports/pirates/inside-the-pirates-the-mvp-that-got-away-497913/

Kovacevic, Dejan. "Pirates confronting the question: Why not Freddy?" Pittsburgh *Post-Gazette*, 26 May 2006. http://www.post-gazette.com/stories/sports/pirates/pirates-confronting-the-question-why-not-freddy-435647/

Lackey, Pat. "Padres 6, Pirates 2." Where Have You Gone, Andy Van Slyke? 23 September 2006. http://whereisvanslyke.blogspot.com/2006/09/padres-6-pirates-2.html

"Matt Morris." FanGraphs.com, Accessed 20 January 2014.
http://www.fangraphs.com/statss.aspx?playerid=1172&position=P

McNulty, Timothy. "Stuffing ballot box for players now part of the All-Star Game routine." Pittsburgh *Post-Gazette*, 25 June 2006. http://www.post-gazette.com/stories/sports/pirates-all-star-game/stuffing-ballot-box-for-players-now-part-of-the-all-star-game-routine-439654/

Meyer, Paul. "Major League Baseball Draft: Pirates select Clemson pitcher in first round." Pittsburgh *Post-Gazette*, 7 June 2007. http://www.post-gazette.com/stories/sports/pirates/major-league-baseball-draft-pirates-select-clemson-pitcher-in-first-round-488432/

Pearlman, Jeff. "Brian Giles is a superstar, but the naked truth is: The rest of this team stinks." *Sports Illustrated*, 25 March 2002. http://sportsillustrated.cnn.com/baseball/mlb/features/2002/scouting_reports/pirates/

Rushin, Steve. "Too true to be good." *Sports Illustrated*, 29 December 2003. http://sportsillustrated.cnn.com/vault/article/magazine/MAG1031003/index.htm

Verducci, Tom. "Beantown bonanza: Red Sox look to complete A-Rod deal to finish off their winter spree." *Sports Illustrated*, 16 December 2003. http://sportsillustrated.cnn.com/2003/writers/tom_verducci/12/16/insider/index.html

Chapter 3

"Basking in reflected glory, cutting off reflected failure, and cutting off future failure: The importance of group identification." Daniel L. Wann, Michael A. Hamlet, Tony A. Wilson, and Joan A. Hodges. *Social Behavior And Personality*. 1995, 23(4): 377-388.

Björkqvist, Kaj. "Social defeat as a stressor in humans." *Psychology and Behavior*. 2001, 73: 435-442. http://www.vasa.abo.fi/svf/up/articles/social_defeat.pdf

Blakeslee, Sandra. "Cells that read minds." The *New York Times*, 10 May 2006. http://www.nytimes.com/2006/01/10/science/10mirr.html?pagewanted=all

Guttmann, Allen. *Sports Spectators*. New York: Columbia University Press, 1986.

Simons, Eric. *The Secret Lives of Sports Fans*. New York and London: Overlook Press, 2013.

Skinner, B.F. *Science and Human Behavior*. New York: Free Press / Simon & Schuster Inc., 1953.

Winegard, Benjamin, and Robert O. Deaner. "The evolutionary significance of Red Sox Nation: Sport fandom as a by-product of coalitional psychology." *Evolutionary Psychology*. 2010, 8(3): 432-446.

Dry Land

http://www.ucweb.gvsu.edu/cms3/assets/6D2549F6-ED41-142A-2D7251DEDEE796B4/deanerfiles/winegard__deaner_2010_the_evolutionary_significance_of_red_sox_nation_-_sport_fandom_as_a_by-product_of_coalitional_psychology.pdf

Chapter 4

Pirates Twitter account, 27 January 2012.
https://twitter.com/Pirates/status/162922728515571712

Chapter 5

Dvorchak, Robert. "Some Bucs fans, but not too many, leave their seats in protest." Pittsburgh *Post-Gazette*, 30 June 2007. http://www.post-gazette.com/stories/sports/pirates/some-bucs-fans-but-not-too-many-leave-their-seats-in-protest-491507/

Forums.MLB.com message-board posting.
http://www.forums.mlb.com/n/pfx/forum.aspx?tsn=6&nav=messages&webtag=ml-pirates&tid=52606. Accessed 6 October 2012.

"The Pirates' McClatchy resigns amid losing year." The Associated Press, 6 July 2007.
http://www.nytimes.com/2007/07/07/sports/baseball/07pirates.html?_r=0

Price, Karen. "'Fans for Change' ready for Pirates protest." Pittsburgh *Tribune-Review*, 27 June 2007.
http://triblive.com/x/pittsburghtrib/sports/pirates/s_514548.html#axzz2TIwOJchH

Young, Chris. "A Conversation with Andy Chomos." Pittsburgh *CityPaper*, 26 July 2007. http://www.pghcitypaper.com/pittsburgh/a-conversation-with-andy-chomos/Content?oid=1338783

Chapter 6

Andrews, Jesse. "It's over cuz you traded McLouth." YouTube, 4 June 2009.
http://www.youtube.com/watch?v=F6ce2-oucmc

Blum, Ronald. "Pirates' payroll at $74.6 million; Yankees hit with luxury tax." The Associated Press, 18 December 2013. http://www.post-gazette.com/sports/pirates/2013/12/18/Pirates-payroll-at-74-6-million-Yankees-hit-with-luxury-tax-again/stories/201312180130

Castrovince, Anthony. "Better late than never, Bautista now the best." MLB.com, 31 May 2011.
http://toronto.bluejays.mlb.com/news/article.jsp?ymd=20110530&content_id=19811258

Crasnick, Jerry. "Pirates 'clean house' in a very big way." ESPN.com, 3 August 2009. http://sports.espn.go.com/mlb/columns/story?columnist=crasnick_jerry&id=4373 943

Creagh, Kevin. "Interview with Frank Coonelly – Follow-up from PirateFest." Pirates Prospects, 21 February 2011. http://www.piratesprospects.com/2011/02/interview-with-frank-coonelly-follow-up-from-piratefest.html

Daquido, comment on "Take 5, Brent Johnson, NFL hypocrisy, 1960 Pirates, Steeler praise." Mondesi's House, 19 October 2010. http://www.mondesishouse.com/2010/10/take-5-brent-johnson-nfl-hypocrisy-1960.html?showComment=1288220010667#c4180494680840452126

Dunlap, Colin. Twitter.com, 25 April 2012. https://twitter.com/colin_dunlap/status/195237419761668096

Kovacevic, Dejan. "Analysis: Why are Brewers outspending Pirates?" Pittsburgh Post-Gazette, 18 April 2007. http://www.post-gazette.com/stories/sports/pirates/analysis-why-are-brewers-outspending-pirates-481487/. Accessed 14 March 2013.

Kovacevic, Dejan. "Wakeup Call: Upgraded farm system?" Pittsburgh Tribune-Review, 28 September 2012. http://blog.triblive.com/dejan-kovacevic/2012/09/28/wakeup-call-upgraded-farm-system/

Langosch, Jenifer. "Pirates' average ticket price to increase in 2012." By gosh, it's Langosch, 30 August 2011. http://langosch.mlblogs.com/2011/08/30/pirates-average-ticket-price-to-increase-in-2012/

"Pittsburgh Pirates." Cot's Baseball Contracts. Accessed 3 January 2014. https://www.baseballprospectus.com/compensation/cots/national-league-central/pittsburgh-pirates/

"Tweak in Bautista's swing contributing to success." Sportsnet, 31 May 2010. http://www.sportsnet.ca/baseball/mlb/going-deep/

Williams, Tim. "Pittsburgh Pirates 2011 40-man roster and payroll." Pirates Prospects, 6 October 2011. http://www.piratesprospects.com/2010/10/2011-pittsburgh-pirates-40-man-roster-and-payroll.html

Williams, Tim. "Pittsburgh Pirates 2012 40-man roster and payroll." Pirates Prospects, 16 October 2012. http://www.piratesprospects.com/2011/10/2012-pittsburgh-pirates-40-man-roster-and-payroll.html

Williams, Tim. "Pittsburgh Pirates 2013 40-man payroll projection. Pirates Prospects. Accessed 3 January 2014. http://www.piratesprospects.com/2013payroll

Wilmoth, Charlie. "Bob Nutting is not a cartoon villain." SB Nation Pittsburgh, 16 August 2010. http://pittsburgh.sbnation.com/2010/8/16/1625105/bob-nutting-is-not-a-cartoon-pirates-john-russell-mlb-draft Bob Smizik's article speculating about

Dry Land

the Pirates firing John Russell appears to have been taken down from the *Post-Gazette* website, but you can find summaries here and elsewhere.

Wilmoth, Charlie. "Nate McLouth traded to Braves." Bucs Dugout, 3 June 2009. http://www.bucsdugout.com/2009/6/3/898128/nate-mclouth-traded-to-braves

Wilmoth, Charlie. "Pirates didn't ask for physical for Akinori Iwamura before trade." Bucs Dugout, 18 June 2010. http://www.bucsdugout.com/2010/6/18/1524713/pirates-didnt-ask-for-physical-for . The Associated Press originally reported the news that the Pirates did not have Iwamura take a physical. Their story seems to have disappeared since then, but I wrote blog posts about it for two separate sites, and Rotoworld.com noted it as well.

Chapter 7

Bowman, Mark. "Umpire Meals: Call 'might have' been wrong." MLB.com, 27 July 2011. http://mlb.mlb.com/news/article.jsp?ymd=20110727&content_id=22363652&vkey=news_mlb&c_id=mlb

Brink, Bill. "Another debacle for Pirates pitchers after 13-2 loss to Padres." Pittsburgh Post-Gazette, 7 August 2011. http://www.post-gazette.com/pirates/2011/08/07/Another-debacle-for-Pirates-pitchers-after-13-2-loss-to-Padres/stories/201108070145

Dunlap, Colin. Twitter.com, 1 March 2011. https://twitter.com/colin_dunlap/status/42719233142030336

"Marlins pitcher Olsen charged with DUI, released from jail." The Associated Press, 22 July 2007. http://sports.espn.go.com/mlb/news/story?id=2944588

Starkey, Joe. "Starkey: Pirates fans waking the dead." Pittsburgh *Tribune-Review*, 23 June 2011. http://triblive.com/x/pittsburghtrib/sports/columnists/starkey/s_743462.html#axzz2hjXxf7zx

Chapter 8

Brink, Bill. "No outside help on offense for now." Pittsburgh *Post-Gazette*, 14 May 2012. http://www.post-gazette.com/stories/sports/pirates/huntington-no-outside-help-on-offense-for-now-635817/

Cooper, J.J. "Scout's view: Pedro Alvarez." *Baseball America*, 17 April 2012. http://www.baseballamerica.com/online/prospects/scouts-view/2012/2613281.html

Kovacevic, Dejan. "Wakeup call: Tower of torture." *TribLIVE Blogs*, 31 July 2012. http://blog.triblive.com/dejan-kovacevic/2012/07/31/wakeup-call-tower-of-torture-2/

Majors, Dan. "Dude, what's the 'Z'? Pirates explain." Pittsburgh *Post-Gazette,* 4 July 2012. http://www.post-gazette.com/pirates/2012/07/04/Dude-what-s-the-Z-Pirates-explain/stories/201207040097

Miller, Wilbur. "Pirates set to downgrade 90-Loss team." Pirates Prospects, 12 October 2011. http://www.piratesprospects.com/2011/10/pirates-set-to-downgrade-90-loss-team.html

Wilmoth, Charlie. "Brewers 10, Pirates 7." Bucs Dugout, 13 July 2012. http://www.bucsdugout.com/2012/7/14/3158511/brewers-10-pirates-7

Wilmoth, Charlie. "Paul Maholm says Pirates did not make offer." Bucs Dugout, 11 January 2012. http://www.bucsdugout.com/2012/1/11/2699224/paul-maholm-says-pirates-did-not-make-offer

Wilmoth, Charlie. "The Pirates aren't out of it. That's not optimism. That's math." Bucs Dugout, 9 September 2012. http://www.bucsdugout.com/2012/9/9/3306165/the-pirates-still-arent-out-of-it-thats-not-optimism-thats-math

Chapter 9

Cameron, Dave. "Why I'm Not a Fan of Losing on Purpose." FanGraphs, 19 November 2012. http://www.fangraphs.com/blogs/index.php/why-im-not-a-fan-of-losing-on-purpose/

Lackey, Pat. "Pirates and Royals: Liveblog." Where Have You Gone, Andy Van Slyke? 20 June 2006. http://whereisvanslyke.blogspot.com/2006/06/pirates-and-royals-liveblog.html

McCauley, Scott. "Is This Possible?" Is This Thing On?, 19 April 2012. http://soisthisthingon.wordpress.com/2012/04/19/is-this-possible/

Wilmoth, Charlie. "In the minor leagues: An interview with Scott McCauley." Bucs Dugout, 27 July 2012. http://www.bucsdugout.com/2012/7/27/3197378/in-the-minor-leagues-an-interview-with-scott-mccauley

Chapter 10

970 ESPN. "David and Mike Happy Hour Seg 2." 22 February 2013. http://www.970espn.com/cc-common/podcast/single_page.html?more_page=1&podcast=David_Todd&selected_podcast=20130222181527_1361576581_20333.mp3

Berardi, Travis. Twitter.com. 1 August 2013. https://twitter.com/TBerardi_OVA/status/363036320207089664

Dry Land

Biertempfel, Rob. "Cole's stellar start gives Pirates' elusive 82nd victory." Pittsburgh *Tribune-Review*, 9 September 2013. http://triblive.com/sports/pirates/4672396-74/pirates-cole-rangers#axzz2eydAR52S

Biertempfel, Rob. "Pirates coaches still learning about Cole." Pittsburgh *Tribune-Review*, 9 June 2013. http://triblive.com/sports/pirates/4166753-74/cole-pirates-coaches#axzz2ocr07Pxt

Calcaterra, Craig. "Pirates fans are coming out of the woodwork." NBC Sports HardballTalk, 8 August 2013. http://hardballtalk.nbcsports.com/2013/08/08/pirates-fans-are-coming-out-of-the-woodwork/

Fuoco, Michael A. "Giant rubber ducky quacking tonight in Pittsburgh." Pittsburgh *Post-Gazette*, 27 September 2013. http://www.post-gazette.com/stories/local/neighborhoods-city/giant-rubber-ducky-will-get-quacking-here-today-705115/

"Game 6: Pirates at Dodgers." *Change in Atmosphere.* 6 April 2013. http://www.changeinatmosphere.com/forum/index.php?showtopic=11686&st=60

Hagen, Paul. "Past Pirates rejoicing in season's success." Pirates.com, 9 September 2013. http://mlb.mlb.com/news/article.jsp?ymd=20130909&content_id=59412368&vkey=news_pit&c_id=pit

Manel, David. "Pirates General Manager Neal Huntington's press conference." Bucs Dugout, 31 July 2013. http://www.bucsdugout.com/2013/7/31/4576646/pirates-general-manager-neal-huntingtons-press-conference

"Pirates acquire Justin Morneau." ESPN News Services, 1 September 2013. http://espn.go.com/mlb/story/_/id/9619812/minnesota-twins-trade-justin-morneau-pittsburgh-pirates

Rosenthal, Ken. Twitter.com. 26 April 2013. https://twitter.com/Ken_Rosenthal/status/327817008156659715

Sanserino, Michael. "Pirates secure first winning season since 1992 with 1-0 win over Rangers." Pittsburgh *Post-Gazette*, 10 September 2013. http://www.post-gazette.com/stories/sports/pirates/pirates-secure-first-winning-season-since-1992-with-1-0-win-over-rangers-702649/

Sanserino, Michael. Twitter.com. 1 October 2013. https://twitter.com/msanserino/status/385250640940646401

Starkey, Joe. "Survival guide for Pirates' fans." Pittsburgh *Tribune-Review*, 21 September 2013. http://triblive.com/sports/joestarkey/4717761-74/baseball-game-games#axzz2fdNV0bFT

Wilmoth, Charlie. "Gerrit Cole's debut a success in 8-2 Pirates win." *Bucs Dugout*, 11 June 2013. http://www.bucsdugout.com/2013/6/11/4421394/gerrit-coles-debut-a-success-in-8-2-pirates-win

Conclusion

Raab, Scott. *The Whore of Akron*. HarperCollins: 2011, 36.

Made in the USA
Charleston, SC
18 March 2014